Th' Callin'

o' Fife

descriptive and ancestral
poetic writing

Robbie Kennedy Bennett

Scottish
Wulfrunian
Poetic Writing of Robbie Kennedy Bennett
since 1989

Th' Callin' o' Fife ©
Robbie Kennedy Bennett 2017

Poetic Writing of Robbie Kennedy Bennett
www.rkbpoetry.co.uk

ISBN-13: 978-1548553364
ISBN-10: 1548553360

Introduction;

Th' Callin' o' Fife is third in line to my writing about my ancestral roots in Scotland. First came **'Wulfrunian Footprints in Fife'** followed by **'Back an' Forth tae Fife.'** They are periods of my writing of what I knew of or found out about at that particular time. It's been a fascinating journey that this laddie from Wolverhampton has travelled, taking into consideration that I was middle age when making my first visit to Fife.

I have on record that I have dated my poetic writing back to 1989. A local nostalgic newspaper The Black Country Bugle were first to print my work leading to Scottish websites displaying me as a featured poet. I had never thought about it really until a reader of books of mine told me that I am greatly influenced by my family. That being so and having ancestral roots in Wolverhampton, Fife and Dundee gave plenty of material to consider.

This poetic writing style of mine comes from a man who was not a great scholar in the classroom; but what I do have is a thoughtful mind which is also needed in my line of work. The sporting background of football and running provides great memories of past times. My wife Lynne and I are grandparents and the books that we have published, this being the seventh, are poetic ancestral journeys that can be revisited.

My first book was **Awa' th' Rough Hills an' Awa'**, my growing up years in ode and story on Rough Hills, Wolverhampton. Next came **Wulfrunian Footprints in Fife**, tracing my roots in Scotland, again in ode and story. **'Ode' Gold Wolves,** poems related to Wolverhampton Wanderers Football Club. All three books were published in less than 3 months. **Kicking around Codsall**, the village where I live, was to follow as was **On a Wolverhampton Journey**, which is my hometown. **Back an' Forth tae Fife** is another ancestral journey which in time may become an important reference or a nice family read for my loved ones.

Poetic Writing of RKB carries on, new ones, old ones, some better than others. The forgotten ones are always a surprise especially if they reach the height of going into a book. At times a new poem flows easy and another is a difficult task.

When collected, put into order, find a photograph and add a descriptive story, the reader can then visualise what you are writing about. **Th' Callin' o' Fife** falls into that ancestral collection of my writing.

My wife Lynne is always a great help when setting up books to assist in taking my writing to the next stage. She must also be drawn to Fife as she always comes with me.

A 'Scottish Wulfrunian Lecture' is a mixture of two of my odes with an additional ending.

A Scottish Wulfrunian Lecture ©

2016

I descend from a working class background;
I grew up in a town of my mothers' line.
I live everyday a Wulfrunian way,
and there is nothing that I want that is not mine.
There are family names scattered all around,
roots of mine are in this town,
within the soil deep in the ground.

And when the daylight in Fife
draws to a close

I reflect on life and of those
who once witnessed the morn
sailed the sea and planted corn
in fields and sea that I look at now
thinking of how you influence
this far away descendant of yours
in awe of the Kingdom
with palette of colours
and lovely tranquil shores

The mind goes back and forth
keeps on going from south to north,
an ancestral vehicle I drive
whilst living, breathing alive.

So when the daylight in Fife
draws to a close
I reflect on life and of those
to meet family names that are scattered around,
in roots of mine that are in this town,
within the soil deep in the Wulfrunian ground.

Aye, they meet in my house and word
in the picturesque process of thought,
brought together, me and mine
locked together in
a Scottish Wulfrunian time.

Eventually the day arrived
saying hello and farewell,
they all spoke at their Scottish Wulfrunian lecture
for me to conjecture and tell.

Content of Odes;

SOLDIER, KIRKCALDY SOLDIER

A Wee Piece o' th' Heart Has the Parish of Dysart

Kinghorn, Look Out For a Wanderer

One Second of Time in The Auld Grey Toun

Nine and Five Eighths of a Mile From Pittenweem

The Greatest Pleasure Was Read

Get Tipsy and Tell yer Scottish Tale

Difficult tae Leave are yer Fife

An April Day in Collessie, Almost a Hogmanay Tale

O John Bennet

An Ode of a Shiny Fife Pound

Climbing Down a Ladder of Past Time in Old Dundee

Children of the Fisher Folk

You Came Back

Kilted by the Tay

The Very Moment of the Reading of Their Name

Kennedy, Trail, Bennet

Duff and Anderson of Kingsbarns

Giffordtown, ay Ye I've Heard

I Gave My All For Cupar Hearts

Ordinary Items Such as Sand and Staine

Come Here Fallen Soldier

A Kirkcaldy Man Named Kennedy

Isabella I Hear You Cry

THE KINGDOM OF FIFE

'Studio Bennetto'

How do I start Th' Callin' o' Fife, good question?

This my third book about my ancestral Scotland but how should it begin?

The magnificent Highlands or Lowlands, Lochs and Glens, William Wallace, Robert the Bruce?

IMAGINABLE DAYS OF ISAIAH OWEN; helps me make the decision to start this latest literary composition of poetic fact and fiction in August 1957 ; when I would be 3 years old; before then let me build up to it. My uncle Ben, moms eldest brother was into photography which is why we have in print a few memories of that time. He must have been at our house on Rough Hills, Wolverhampton where my elder brother Gareth and myself were in the so called 'Studio Bennetto' for a photographic session. There's me looking at the ceiling on a toy rocking horse with the description 'Robbie rides the range on a galloping steed.'

Mom was the youngest of the Owen children of All Saints and unfortunately her mother died within a few weeks of her being born. Her parents were Benjamin James Owen and Sarah Ann Williams who married in the church of All Saints in 1915. We have a history of starting our education years next door where the school buildings still stand but is no more. Sarah Ann's parents Joseph Williams and Sarah Ann Darby also married at All Saints in 1893.

All Saints was a typical tight knit community of that time with terraced houses, shops, pubs, factories and a workhouse. One such place of work was Edge Tools which I imagine employed many folk from the surrounding area. We were industrial and an employee would be a great grandfather of mine named Isaiah Owen.

Imaginable days of Isaiah Owen ©
Robbie Kennedy Bennett

Imaginable days of Isaiah Owen ©

2016

I took that picture today, I took a picture.....

We were industrial I can tell
probably had a life as tough as hell,
as fellow Wulfrunians as well,
we needed to be industrial.

We were industrial
many worked I see at Edge Tool,

survival I imagine did rule.
Bilston Road, Eagle works
sometimes it kind of hurts to be close
for I found there was a workhouse,
thinking of situations in mind
brings a sorry feeling of some kind.

I see the year of 1838
built to accommodate 750 an inmate,
male, female, young or old
was it overcrowded, strict and cold?

Young Isaiah Owen
you must have seen a workhouse child or two,
and I wonder if the workhouse children
when on Eagle Street or Bilston Road
perhaps Isaiah, they saw you.

Aye, young Isaiah Owen
iron you rolled and forged your career,
you became a widower
into a second marriage your life did steer.

The First World War
Gt Britain before the First World War,
today Eagle Street has a different feel

early Sunday in my branded trainers,
not a worn out soul and heel.

On this map I see there was a chapel
at the corner with Bilston Road,
was it all in agreement, welcomed
or perhaps complaints
with changes to Monmore Green and All Saints.

O'er the other side of the Bilston Road
on the bridge I stare,
Isaiah Owen, did you ever stand
where I'm standing there?

I press search to find an address,
avoiding making an accidental ancestral mess,
one cannot deter
visualising how important the waterways were.

'Back of Eagle Works,' was one
another, was it your father at 'Canal Side'
near to Edge Tool Company
on the towpath barges were tied

In the days of young Isaiah Owen
digging, shovelling and hoeing

tools made by his father
on the canal they were going.

We were industrial
around this area we strode,
marriages, births and deaths
probably buried in Merridale,
Jeffcock Road.

At aged 15, myself a working teen
at old EP Jenks, then Delta Rods
at the time of Skinheads,
Rockers and Mods.

Yet to know, or be interested
in days a long time ago,
manufacturing a spade, shovel or hoe
would later bother me so,
the days of an elderly Isaiah Owen
knowing another Benjamin, his son
to fight in France he would be going.

I worked within a half of a mile
in fact a few feet in sight for a while,
the canal nearby, where my hard working Wulfrunians
were underneath the same Wulfrunian sky.

Best suit, a Sunday dress, grown ups, a hardworking teen,
a King and Queen, coronation time they've seen
Wolverhampton town, All Saints and Monmore Green.

Isaiah Owen, your dad put his mark
he couldn't write, but I bet he could work
from morning to night, aye until dark,
can't see him as a fool,
Benjamin Owen, the hoe maker at Edge Tool.

We were industrial, no more than that,
I bet we could graft at the drop of a hat,
miners, colliers, the barge fills
of coal from a seam on the Rough Hills.

Isaiah Owen, whilst in your fifties
came your last breath
your son named Edward
was present at your death.

You were still working oh Isaiah Owen
no surprising at Edge Tool,
you can't call it old age poor Isaiah
pneumonia so cruel.

We were industrial
on the back of the revolution,
the solution to be alive and survive
was to be industrial.

We were industrial
around this area we strode,
marriages, births and deaths
probably buried in Merridale,
Jeffcock Road, we toiled,
I imagine our hands were soiled,
because we needed to be industrial.

I took that picture today, I take a picture,
the workhouse I write of is long gone
the canal is quieter Isaiah these days,
picturing a window in the Victorian era
and an imaginary child did wave Isaiah
an imaginary child did wave.

Watching me take a picture today, take a picture.....

Because of the sad start in life that mom had she was
adopted by her newly married aunt and uncle into the
Rowley family who became our much loved nan and
grandad. Mom and dad met whilst in Aldershot Military
Hospital and settled in her home town of Wolverhampton.
Dad was from Ladybank in Fife, Scotland. In recent years I
have been exploring our roots in which I wish it had been
done earlier in life; meaning in his lifetime so he could have
added factual detail to this story.

My two previous books relevant to Scotland, firstly
'Wulfrunian Footprints in Fife' and then 'Back an' Forth tae
Fife' were both featured in the FIFE FREE PRESS weekly
newspaper. They explain briefly the poetic story of how I
keep on finding the heart and desire to drive up to Fife to
unearth family history.

Going back to the start of this book, I am riding that
galloping steed all the way from 'Studio Bennetto' on Rough
Hills to South Queensferry. The journey was long and tiring
so we rested by the banks of the Firth of Forth. It is August
1957 and before the road bridges were built. This time
instead of looking at the ceiling of the 'Studio Bennetto' it is
at an image of Scotland that I will see many times in years
to come.

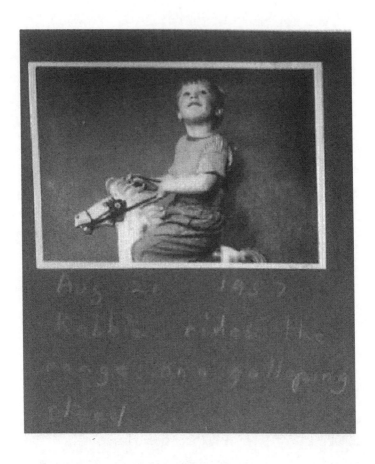

There was some kind of a calling inside of me to go over to the land across the water. A ferry arrives and I hear a voice shout "is 'at ye Wulfrunian laddie? Before I could answer the ferryman said "yer tae suin laddie, tae suin." So we turned around and galloped on home to the Rough Hills.

'we were never really in danger
safe was this Rough Hills Ranger!
to live to tell the story
more ordinary than battles and glory'

Could Be The Iconic Image of Scotland

'the oldest, aye you're old,
yet still I am in awe
excited at the sight'

Whenever in South Queensferry I look over to Fife and experience a belonging feeling. I would have travelled many a mile and longed for plenty of times to be near the Forth. There my ancestral home reaches out and grabs my attention. I should imagine that many a Fifer from past time watched the magnificent Victorian structure become what we know today.

My family line, for those who don't know, on one side were from Ladybank and one young man by the name of Thomas Loch Traill Bennet died in a motorcycle accident in 1933. On his death certificate his profession was a bridge painter. I can't help but wonder if the Forth Rail Bridge was ever a place of work for him.

Studying a black and white photograph from 1931 of painters in flat cap and jackets walking up a cantilever of the Forth Bridge. Head down and concentrating on their next step as one mistake could prove to be fatal. When at rest what magnificent views they would have seen.

It may be that the photographer is on the cantilever nearest South Queensferry as the uninhibited Isle of Inchgarvie is below the previous one. This island helps form the foundation of the middle cantilever. I searched for a photo of mine to study some more and found myself imagining those painters in 1931 on that picture of mine in 2013.

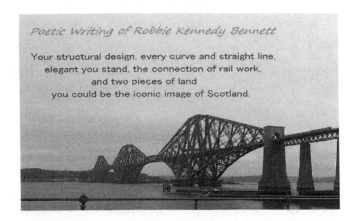

Poetic Writing of Robbie Kennedy Bennett

Your structural design, every curve and straight line,
elegant you stand, the connection of rail work,
and two pieces of land
you could be the iconic image of Scotland.

Could be the Iconic Image of Scotland ©

2016

The oldest, aye you're old, yet still I am in awe
excited at the sight
even though my eyes have been set on you
so many times before.

I look for you, searching landscape
in the near approaching mile,
joy, as a match winner for a while
aye a classic example of a particular style.

Your structural design, every curve and straight line,
elegant you stand, the connection of rail work,

and two pieces of land
you could be the iconic image of Scotland.

Would I have wanted to help make you in the 1880's?
Now there's something worth talking,
or to be one of those brave painters
along a cantilever walking,
challenging weather, team work, together,

Dawn until light fades
close comrades you appear,
not frightened of heights, no fear,
nerves of the same steel,
the same steel you are painting,
what could be the iconic image of Scotland.

Still in awe, aye you're old
you must feel magnificently cold
when fortunately close to touch,
such a historical journey
this rhyme of mine does drive,
you brush stroking bridge painters
no longer alive, dangerously working to survive.

Time brings change, risks are less,
safety at work they address,
still hard to believe, flat cap, winter jacket,

heat, rolled up sleeve.
South and North Queensferry, Lothian and Fife looking on
down
they brushed up and smartened
what could be the iconic image of Scotland.

In modern time you have what can be called company
spanning both Queensferry's, three I see,
stand proud, auld lassie don't frown or put yourself down,
you could be the iconic image of Scotland.

The Forth Belle disembarked its sightseeing passengers at South Queensferry. We stood there with our tea in polystyrene cups taking in the tranquil setting by the Forth Rail Bridge. There we were once again, 'last of the big spenders.' The water lapped against the wall making a soothing sound which drew your mind into this calm setting. Then came the rumbling entrance from up above as a train coming from Dalmeny Station passed over the bridge. This trip was just in time for Lynne and myself as there had been a couple of health issues for the both of us.

The new Queensferry crossing is nearing completion and draws the attentive eye from the Victorian rail bridge when driving over the Forth. There is plenty of roadwork alterations either side therefore concentration is important.

Ballingry,
Oh Ballingry

'emotions are always high
standing bemused beneath a Fife sky'

One more visit to Fife and once again I stand looking at a gravestone of who in ancestral terms is my grandmother. It has only been just over a year since first experiencing that feeling that has now become ritual that I have to do. We may be a family unknown to her other offsprings and that's what we have to live with. Nevertheless my respect is paid every time.

Ballingry, Oh Ballingry

Ballingry, Oh Ballingry ©

2016

Raised upon the Rough Hills
with an All Saints education
I live in Staffordshire by Codsall Station
with a strong temptation to share
my time with my roots elsewhere.

All over the place my mind plays

when near All Saints, my All Saints days,
expecting the same on Steelhouse Lane,
something calls again and there it stays.

Always prods me gently when about here
where my mother was born,
reminding I'm somewhere near,
I feel it so, embracing it, don't want to let that feeling go.

How come, when I drive around Lochgelly
and to Ballingry, how come,
how come when I'm about Lochore,
and I yearn to come again some more,
how come, oh how come?

I'd moved on more than fifty years
then another calling in life appears,
half a century of living,
how come Fife, how come?

Ballingry you didn't know me then,
neither did Lochgelly, when I was ten,
your wait has suited me fine
from Rough Hills and All Saints
and a laddie of nine,
Ballingry, oh Ballingry.

Lochore Meadows Country Park
I see me running 'till the day comes dark,
hot summer and winter chill
I'd love to see snow on Benarty Hill
how come Fife, how come?

From my Rough Hills to
Lochore Meadows Country Park
imagining men and times of the working mines,
I rest aside Loch Ore
thinking of those old miners
of Rough Hills and Fife before
how come Fife, how come?

Ballingry, oh Ballingry
not knowing me as a laddie of seven or eight,
let's say it's never too late
Ballingry, oh Ballingry.

Sometimes findings can weigh a ton
then not even an ounce,
how come once I step foot in Fife
ancestral feelings they pounce?

Emotions are always high

standing bemused beneath a Fife sky,
I get the feeling that
I'd won and lost in Ballingry
Ballingry, oh Ballingry.

Driving away from Ballingry
into a Perth and Kinross scene,
which is impressive, worth finding,
a pleasure to have seen
that Perth and Kinross scene
and Ballingry, oh Ballingry.

Ballingry and onto Ladybank was the plan of ours then finding somewhere for lunch. We ended up at the Harbour Cafe in Tayport which is also a Welcome Port on the Fife Coastal Path.

I took a photograph looking down Dalgleish Street wondering what dwelling my Bennet's lived in when first coming to Fife in the early 1900's. Hector and Isabella were newly married and their first child was born here. I didn't know of him and found him quite accidentally living out his life in Australia. I was to lay awake early two mornings later in St Andrews with the Bennet children and their eventual leaving of Fife heavily on my mind. It's remarkable that they left Fife behind for me to arrive and embrace it.

Tayport was peaceful and quiet this sunny Sunday afternoon with glorious views over the Tay to the Angus coast. Earlier we had stopped at a viewing point looking over to Dundee. My mind went back to when I was nearing the end when walking the coastal path. Once again I looked at the bridge knowing that soon I would be crossing into the city of culture and my ancestral past; the mind plays games.

*Soon after it was a drive o'er
into the 19th Century
the mind plays games,
oh Bonnie Dundee,
the mind plays games with me....*

My Pride in The Tay

*'forefathers wudnae a' seen
a different day, a different realm,
king or queen'*

Later that afternoon we had settled into the Invercarse Hotel on the Perth Road. From the dining room and the tables outside is a glimpse of a view of the Tay. Dundee airport is on the riverside and the engines of the planes were heard soon to see the taking of flight. The Tay and setting of Dundee would be very much the same as my ancestors day but modern living is influential in its character. A welcome pint and an outside table was appreciated with many a thought of changes to Dundee but how the Tay stays the same. Plans were to early next morning get to the top of The Law.

This man, born in Wolverhampton with a Fife and Dundee ancestral interest, from the height of The Law he looked down into his past. My Bennet, Anderson, Traill and more of my ancestors were with me, it was a proud feeling.

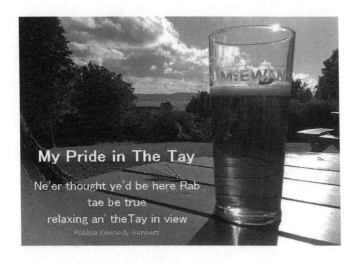

My Pride in The Tay ©

2016

Ne'er thought ye'd be here Rab tae be true
relaxing an' the Tay in view
talking 'bout thinking before
aye nineteen hundred and two.

Dundonian forefathers
relied on world trade what the Tay supplied,
I tried for an age or two, I tried
to engage with Dundonuan forefathers, I tried.

I take pride, for a minute or two, I take pride
from the Tay where on they relied,
to live and eat, have shoes on their feet
clothes on their Dundonian frame
the Tay stays the same.

Watching planes take flight
taking flight from left to right,
forefathers wudnae a' seen
a different day, a different realm, king or queen.

Buildings built, grown fast
jute factories unifies the Dundee past,
street signs for the industry remain
only the Tay stays the same.

She stays the same
eyes to the Tay they aim,
her water I feel the power
September breeze, afternoon hour,
Dundonian forefathers, proud that I came
only the Tay stays the same.

Dundonian forefathers
aye you, who I carry your name,

only the Tay stays the same
that reasoning I applied
for a while I do, I take pride
I take pride from the Tay, I take pride.

Ne'er thought ye'd be here Rab tae be true
relaxing on the Law an' the Tay in view,
talking 'bout thinking before
nineteen hundred and two.

Yesterday I climbed The Law
longed a lang time for one day to do,
I caught the sun at dawn
once more I feel a Dundonian re-born.

Dundonian forefathers
I toast your hard Dundee life,
with the Tay in view
an' the coast of Fife

I take pride in the Tay I take pride
they relied on the Tay they relied,
aside of the Tay there aside
I take pride in the Tay I take pride

Hang up yer Boots Rab on a Silverbirch in Scotland

'and I'm bound to be I'm bound,
to be running around, running around
with the Law in the background'

As you approach Dundee from Fife you can't help but notice that the city isn't built on flat land. In fact it is quite a dramatic rise in height with what is called the Law. This means hill so anyone referring to Law hill is factually wrong. I have often seen photographs from the Law overlooking Dundee and wanted to be up there myself to add to my list of Scottish experiences.

As we were ordering our Sunday evening meal at the hotel

this friendly waitress told us that Dundee Football Club
were holding an event in the ballroom. She was a supporter
of the dark blues and told us that all the players were here. I
had noticed a number of cars arriving earlier and rightly so
next morning there were a few players down at breakfast.

The approach to the Law is a steady rise of housing estates
with a ten minute or so of paths and steps. I was on a short
timescale as breakfast that I mentioned at the Invercarse
Hotel was until nine thirty. Studying a map early that
morning showed that I could drive up and park quite near.
There was one photo stop on the drive up and that was at
Lochee Park with football pitches and the Law in the
background. One imagined if any promising youngsters
had started on their footballing path playing on that field
that stopped me in my tracks.

Hang Up Yer Boots Rab on a Silverbirch in Scotland ©
Poetic Writing of Robbie Kennedy Bennett

Hang Up Yer Boots Rab
on a Silverbirch in Scotland ©

2016

A Silverbirch and a football pitch
and the Law in the background,
'seems sound to me seems sound
and I'm bound to be I'm bound,
to be running around, running around
with the Law in the background'
Aye, that's what I thought

like a fish in a river I was caught,
goalposts came to my attention
in this fictional story poem I should mention;
'that a Silverbirch and a football pitch
and the Law in the background,'
'seems sound to me seems sound
and I'm bound to be I'm bound,
to be running around, running around
with the Law in the background'
If a laddie that's what I would do
doing my best to play in a shirt dark blue,
Dens Park, the next step in the game for me
running on out and scoring a goal for The Dee.
'that Silverbirch and a football pitch
and the Law in the background,'
'seems sound to me seems sound
and I'm bound to be I'm bound,
to be running around, running around
with the Law in the background'
Sadly, those younger days are past
pleasingly my imaginative mind
makes my playing day last,
it's just a tree and a pitch
and a goal where Rab could score,
but those days are gone
and Rab's here to climb the Law;

'just a Silverbirch and a football pitch
and the Law in the background,'
If I had one wish my friend,
this is where my playing day should end,
in respect of my Scottish roots
where I'd be hanging up my boots.
'though it hurts somewhat
go back, I cannot,
still this strange old mind does search.
because of goalposts and a Silverbirch.
On that Silverbirch by a football pitch
and the Law in the background,'
imagine yer boots Rab tied around
oh so tightly....
'seems sound to me seems sound.'

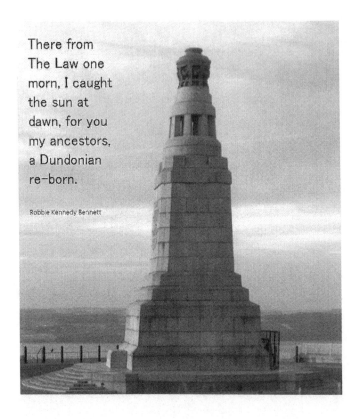

There from
The Law one
morn, I caught
the sun at
dawn, for you
my ancestors,
a Dundonian
re-born.

Robbie Kennedy Bennett

There from The Law one morn, I caught the sun at dawn,
for you my ancestors, a Dundonian re-born.

I was soon at the summit of Dundee Law having driven my car and parked near Lawton Road. I saw an opening that appeared to be the popular path. There was signs of a 'Friends of Dundee Law' meeting fixed to posts that prevent vehicle access. Soon the first sighting of the magnificent war memorial was in view. The unveiling to commemorate the citizens of Dundee who lost their life in the 1914-18 war was made in 1925.

I looked down on the city and views of the bridges and over to Fife and strong feelings of my Scottish ancestry surfaced. I'm fortunate to have known and found family history in both Wolverhampton and Scotland and once again another memorable moment was experienced.

I wasn't alone on the summit as there was a photographer with his apparatus set-up to catch the dawn in picture. His name was Steve from Dundee Prints and we got chatting for a few minutes. He was soon away as he needed to be back home to do the school run. I did find his page on Facebook and pressed 'like' to a picture that he had posted. I couldn't help but admire Steve's passion in photography to capture those special moments.

Our first full day in St Andrews was spent in meeting up with Paul who is a Wolverhampton cousin of mine. After a couple of cups of tea in the caravan it was a walk down to town. Paul is a caddie on the Old Course and has lived up here for well over a decade. He took us to the university museum which is past the castle ruins towards the West Sands and has fabulous views from the terrace enhanced by a telescope. I have to admit that we didn't know of this museum and it was a worthwhile delightful visit. Later Paul caught a bus to Leuchars with arrangements made to come over to the caravan later with his partner Jacqui. Weather wise this was to be our best day as high winds and showers were blowing in.

It was a beast of a wind that built up throughout the afternoon and evening to reach its height overnight. Upon opening the caravan door I could see that one of the aluminium patio chairs had been blown to the end of the decking. If it wasn't for the fencing it may have been blown over to Kingsbarns towards the East Neuk. Down by the entrance to the coastal path I could see that someone's patio double seating was also a victim of the wind with it lying upside down a few yards away from its decking opening. I could see that there was not a gate therefore on a stronger gale it could one day be further afield or even into St Andrews Bay.

Names on stones in the cathedral ruins and Eastern Cemetery still draw my attention and I find over the years forgetting as much as I am learning. Trail, Brown, Buddo, Gourlay, Wallace, Mearns, Elder and more get me wondering if we have a connection.

Back at the caravan with a cup of tea outside I look down on the spires of the auld grey toun and wonder if I have missed anything or anyone. Were there signs that I hadn't picked up on?

*'You're out there,
out there somewhere
aye somewhere,
somewhere out there'*

It wasn't a good forecast so we decided to drive to Perth to do some shopping. The Cupar to Newburgh road is one that I am not familiar with so it was a change to admire a different landscape. Whilst we were doing so and just past Dunbog Primary School, Lynne caught sight of a film crew in the field. They appeared to be setting up to interview someone.

We parked up just outside the city near North Inch park, where the Battle of the Clans took place in September 1396. This was fought out in front of spectators that included King Robert III of Scotland. Sir Walter Scott in The Fair Maid of Perth writes a bloody, gruesome vivid account of how the clans fought whilst bagpipes played out.

I had it in my mind that Lynne didn't enjoy Perth but apparently not as a good couple of hours was spent around the shops. We were accompanied on our last visit by our mothers and can recall walking all the way to the Black Watch Museum to find it not open. It was a ten minute walk back to the car and rain was now drizzling quite a bit. At least the two umbrellas that I had in the boot of the car weren't getting wet!

I have previously mentioned in my books that we have either a Bennet link to Angus or Perthshire. When studied both seem possible and it does lie a wee bit uneasy on my mind not knowing which is the correct line. In the Perthsire claim John Bennet my ggg grandfather from Luncarty was the son of Hector Bennet and Ann Stewart.

A WEE VERSE FOR
MY AIN FOLK

'down Baker Lane
walking with
Wallace and Millar again'

Next morning as I walked by the East Sands at St Andrews a
rainbow appeared to be making a great effort in being seen.

The actual end in my view was the cathedral ruins therefore if I have any fortune to find then it must be there. Wishful thinking as it was Thursday morning when I always put the lottery on.

It was 'hold on to the caravan door time.' We were into over two days of extremely strong winds which did not show this morning in the coastal photographs. Grey and blue sky as the sun was making an appearance and also clear views of Angus. Autumn fields of different colours were quite visible along that coastline which would have been seen countless times by my forefathers. It was also a coast that I have walked having got as far as Arbroath.

I stopped and studied both sides of the East Gate arch, a shield of somekind in the stone is still partly visible. For a moment I wandered back in time and could imagine many an ancestor of mine walking under the same archway heading for town. It was noticeable that the high wind dropped when stepping away up towards the gate at the Eastern Cemetery. There was almost a still of calmness putting a different feel to my morning.

It's strange when you see the same surnames of friends past and present on stones. I immediately bring those people into mind and two such names were side by side which transported me back to time that I spent with them.

Back at the caravan on Kinkell Braes waiting for the high winds to die down as forecast, I write this paragraph on a sunny decking. I can tell that the North Sea in St Andrews Bay is choppy and surprisingly I can see spectators on the top of St Rules Tower! Hold on tight folks!

I recited a wee verse for my ain folk;

"down Baker Lane
walking with
Wallace and Millar again,
expecting to meet;
nae, more wanting to meet
a Brown or Traill
on South Castle Street"

We put off going a ride out until the afternoon as the forecast was for the high wind was to ease. I was having thoughts that I should be out there experiencing the challenges that Fife delivers. We agreed on Lynne staying in the caravan reading her book and yours truly going walking. It was a coastal path decision and in the opposite direction that I normally take. From out on the Kinkell Braes I headed for the Rock and Spindle. It is a volcanic plug rock formation down by the sea a short distance away from the ancient town.

I soon realised that I had become to accustomed to the same view as they came quick and fast to me. Strangely it brought back old memories that had lay deep in me of my coastal walk in 2008. Steps that I had once walked up were challenging my older joints going back down. I had aged and didn't I know it as I thought that I should have brought with me a walking stick of some kind to give me support. I felt a long way away from being that 3 hour marathon man from the mid 1980's. A dozen thoughts came to mind but what won over is that Fife and her views from where I was looked grand.

The shelter amongst the wild shrubs and fern was welcoming and it was good to be outside. Steps had hand made criss cross patterns on showing the efforts of the coastal path workers.

The Rock and Spindle came into view which once again

brought dormant memories, all be it from the opposite direction. I took a few photos from the St Andrews side but really wanted to take one or two from the other side with the sun behind me. When doing so and to my surprise I found another coastal path walker having a mid day nap up against the very rock formation that I had made the effort to get to. I wasn't annoyed in any way but amused as it made an interesting fact to my story.

I turned around for my walk back to Kinkell Braes thinking of the young man named Duff who survived but his brother and their friend didn't. This was long before my day but the journey was very much the same except that he had got to announce the fatalities if it wasn't known already.

A Bonnie Grandaughter Likeness, That Lass on the Harbour Wall

'then this young lass
she walked the harbour wall'

It was our final day in St Andrews and I decided to walk to the end of the harbour wall. The stones are laid in two levels with seating points along the way. Apparently much of the wall is made from cathedral ruins.

The town because of the university has many students and most mornings I see them out jogging. It was noticeable that some of the younger generation walk the higher part of the harbour wall. For a while I was at the furthest point watching the sunrise and the tide coming in. Soon the harbour will be filled and lobster boats can get themselves out in the bay.

I made my way back with views of the cathedral ruins and could see a young student walking towards me on the higher part. I glanced and couldn't help but notice that although a bit older she had a likeness to a grandaughter of mine. A few seconds later when turning around I could still see her walking towards the sunrise.

An immediate parental thought came to mind with having youngsters away from home. St Andrews University has students from many a far off town or city.

Wouldn't it be coincidental and definitely wonderful if my grandchildren or their children were to be students in St Andrews? Wearing that red robe and walking along that harbour wall?

No matter what, they shall have my utmost love and pride. Aaron, Liam, Kiera-Marie, Caitlyn, Jacob and soon to be born Lucas (parents Steven & Teri and brother to Shani)

I often wonder if a car or two or perhaps a mini bus will travel the journey north with those on board to Fife. Some have already done so and here's me thinking ahead and imagining them following my miles and footsteps.

Futuristic thinking; it's a pleasant sunny afternoon in St Andrews, one of those mentioned is now an adult relaxing at a pavement cafe table collecting the warmth of the day in their Scottish Wulfrunian face. They are wearing fashionable sunglasses; their eyes are closed and they think of me and feel their belonging to Fife and St Andrews. The company they are with have listened to their ancestral story and they are impressed, envious even; they all return the next day, at another table and think the very same thoughts.

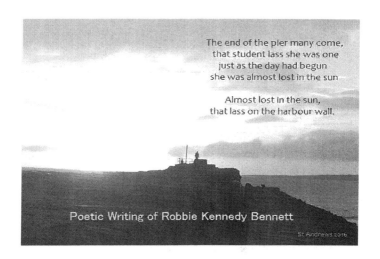

The end of the pier many come,
that student lass she was one
just as the day had begun
she was almost lost in the sun

Almost lost in the sun,
that lass on the harbour wall.

Poetic Writing of Robbie Kennedy Bennett

St Andrews 2016

A Bonnie Grandaughter Likeness ,
That Lass on the Harbour Wall ©

2016

Sunrise is here
thoughts of Friday departure I steer,
time is getting increasingly near
to the leaving of St Andrews.

The tide was rolling in

as I was rolling out,
soon to be rolling on out
out of the auld grey toun

Attracted to Fridays sunrise
there the old body does rise,
newly awakened old eyes
attracted to another sunrise.

The furthest point of that pier
feeling there's so much that's going on here,
sunrise and tide they relate
old and new feelings create.

I decided to ride the tide
decided to turn around,
decided to leave the sight and sound
and get to the auld grey toun.

Then this young lass
she walked the harbour wall
'a Bonnie grandaughter likeness'
high on the harbour wall.

She made me stall
that student lass on the wall,

a thought came across should I call?
I let it pass to that lass on the harbour wall.

She walked the harbour wall
making her taller than I,
beyond her I registered colours
on a palette of a grey sky

Perhaps she's a long way from home
there brings another concern,
'a Bonnie grandaughter likeness'
forcing my head to turn.

The end of the pier many come,
that student lass she was one
just as the day had begun
she was almost lost in the sun

Almost lost in the sun,
that lass on the harbour wall.

Caught by a rainbow appearance
grey clouds refused to make clearance,
into the trees at Tentsmuir
and on golden sand for sure.

The tide was rolling in
as I was rolling out,
soon to be rolling on out
out of the auld grey toun

And that young lass
she walked back on the harbour wall,
my polite "good morning"
a pleasant answer of "hi" that's all.

Of course I dare not call
'you've a Bonnie grandaughter likeness'
don't wish to cause alarm after all
upon that lass from the harbour wall.

'a Bonnie grandaughter likeness'
towards Kirk Hill she did go,
from there on I did not know,
she went away, away she did so,
and away with Fridays rainbow.

Sunrise is here
thoughts of Friday departure I steer,
down to Dumfries and Galloway
then home the next day.

An inner feeling caring call
"be careful lass, don't fall"
careful, is a kindred feeling, after all

Upon walking down the Pends and into the harbour I
noticed another student doing stretching exercise against
the steel harbour railings. I assumed that he was preparing
for going jogging until suddenly he leapt up and was
balancing on the railings with both feet. He was obviously a
gymnast and after our short lighthearted conversation
about me not going to try it, he told me he was of Scottish
family born and raised in the Netherlands. We said our
goodbye and I saw him last somersaulting over an East
Sands bench.

We had tea and a scone down in lovely Culross as it was a
must visit of mine that there was a dwelling called Bennet
House. I had found it on a Fife newsfeed as they were
renovating the building. There's no known connection of
mine but the very name drew me to it.

Later in the afternoon we checked into our guest house in
Dumfries. We had been held back for half an hour because

of an accident on the M74. Our room in Dumfries Villa overlooked St John the Evangelist church and the war memorial. The lone soldier stands with rifle grounded on the handle and his head bowed.

As always I read every name in search of a Scottish Bennet or Kennedy. Coincidently there are two Private James Kennedy's, one of the Gordon Highlanders and the other the 1st Battalion, Kings Own Scottish Borders. I don't think for a minute that they are family of any kind as Kennedy's were known to be in the south west of Scotland.

Interestingly I found a picture of the unveiling ceremony where the granite stone looks snow white in the black and white photograph surrounded by hundreds of spectators.

It could be a reason to delaying my leaving of Scotland that we headed for Gretna Green for a shopping stop. I recalled quite clearly the last time we were here with grandchildren Liam and Kiera as we had a picnic on the grass at the back of the car. After purchasing a few gifts for the grandchildren it was time to head south. As we came to the crossroads to turn right towards Gretna I noticed the piper crossing the road to go to work. It was Saturday and he would playing for the bride and groom and their weddings.

I checked my drivers side mirror as I entered the southbound junction of the motorway. All was clear in front and behind and in the reflection I caught sight of the Saltire on the northward side. I glanced once or twice at that sign and watched it go out of sight, thus ending another Scottish chapter of ours.

Within a couple of weeks of my return I was to be offered the opportunity to go there on work related business.

THE OLD SCOTTISH STONE ©

Robbie Kennedy Bennett

9th June 2002

What should I be thinking?

Or should I say,

As I stand on the coast

At St Andrews Bay.

Today I'm Awa' tae Scotland

*'In darkness of this room
in the lightness of this living'*

It's the end of October 2016 and the clocks have been set back at the end of British Summertime. I'm packed and ready and beginning to wake as plans have been made to go to Scotland. This time it is a work related trip just as that one made in 2002 which unearthed feelings that produced my writing 'The Old Scottish Stone.'

Lying in my room awakening slowly with my dad heavily on my mind. It was 30 years gone last January since I last saw him in the living world, but I see him today in the imagining one and he's laughing and smiling that I'm soon to be going to Scotland.

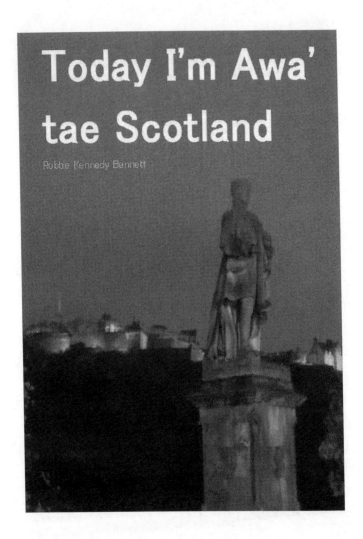

Today I'm Awa'
tae Scotland

Robbie Kennedy Bennett

Today I'm Awa' tae Scotland ©

2006

I see you smiling, I hear you laughing, I know you're

pleased

'cause today I'm awa' tae Scotland.

The clocks went back just now

and so did this life in ways

back to my days in childhood

o'er fifty years in time.

I see you smiling, I hear you laughing, I know you're

pleased

'cause today I'm awa' tae Scotland.

In darkness of this room

in the lightness of this living,

words are written, obviously smitten,

"a laddie's going, aye going soon"

I see you smiling, I hear you laughing, I know you're

pleased

'cause today I'm awa' tae Scotland.

my case is packed with a lifetime and more,

you watch me dress and walk out of my door.

I see you smiling, I hear you laughing,

I know you're pleased

'cause today I'm awa' tae Scotland.

awa' a few hours awa', aye today I'm awa' tae Scotland,

The Half Ay Fife
That You Refuse
tae Let Go

'I saw you as seeing a son or a daughter,
I saw you o'er the water,
o'er the water there'

For once in a long time I was a passenger on route to
Scotland. It was an early morning pick-up for me as the
lack of sleeping hours had been compensated with the
adjustment of the clocks.

Later that morning I was at the Forth Rail Bridge marvelling
once again at the magnificent structure. Queensferry
Crossing has came on massively since Lynne and I were

staying at the Ferry Hotel in 2015. The approach road on the south side is taking shape and the imagination of taking that route one day was made. The Forth was calm and for my colleague it was his first close up sighting of the bridge. Soon photographs were taken and sent to family members who replied in seconds because of modern technology at its best. For me it was a view and my ancestral Fife was calling.

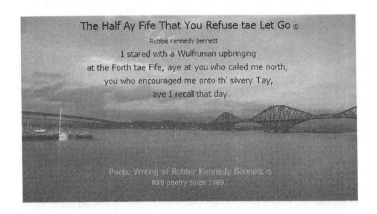

The Half Ay Fife That You Refuse tae Let Go ©
Robbie Kennedy Bennett
I stared with a Wulfrunian upbringing
at the Forth tae Fife, aye at you who called me north,
you who encouraged me onto th' silvery Tay,
aye I recall that day.

Poetic Writing of Robbie Kennedy Bennett ©
RKB poetry since 1989

The Half Ay Fife
That You Refuse tae Let Go ©

2016

I stared with a Wulfrunian upbringing
at the Forth tae Fife, aye at you who called me north,
you who encouraged me onto th' silvery Tay,
aye I recall that day.
Now tae this day, I saw you o'er the water
I saw you as seeing a son or a daughter,
I saw you o'er the water, o'er the water there.
You draw my eyes, my heart you find,
and of course you remind me of me and how I've grown
there's a half of me you own, that you're alway clinging,

clinging to me, regardless of my Wulfrunian upbringing.
There's a half of me that you own,
and I feel ay Fife you have known
is the half ay Fife that you refuse tae let go.
Mother called, father so, as the fabulous Forth,
ay the Forth, as you well know, she sweetly does flow.

Our work related business took us to Heriot-Watt
University in Edinburgh and later that day I was hear the
National Anthem of Flower of Scotland being played.

The following day we travelled to Hibernian FC's training
ground at Ormiston, East Lothian where my colleague and I
were guests. My football knowledge is of Hibs' Famous Five;
Gordon Smith, Bobby Johnstone, Lawrie Reilly, Eddie
Turnbull and Willie Ormond.

Lucas
in the East Lothian
Sunrise of Gold

*'come Friday there's a light westerly
wind, overnight, feeling cold,*

*one day later,
meeting a new grandson one day old'*

A lovely morning view from my hotel window was a joy to
see. I have in my family tree a connection to Edinburgh but
that was in the 1700's. It must be said that I was in some
great company during this time.

Fife was on my mind greatly as I was only a short journey
away, also Lynne and I were soon to be grandparents once
again.

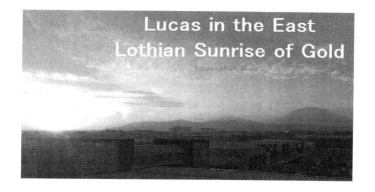

Lucas

in the East Lothian Sunrise of Gold ©

2016

Last week it was Edinburgh
and the gold Lothian sunrise
no surprise, aye no surprise,
I enjoyed the Lothian sunrise.

One day later, I'm heading on back
one day later, I'm heading on back o'er the border,
the Scottish English border, heading on back.

Come Friday there's a light westerly wind,
overnight, feeling cold,

one day later,
meeting a new grandson one day old,
one day it was Edinburgh, Lothian sunrise of gold,
Pentland Hills, one day it was Sunday,
a new grandson, one day old.

Lucas, on your day there are fireworks and fires
this an annual commemoration,
now it's a family celebration for life of a boy
look and listen,
share the British tradition and enjoy.

Lucas, bright or shining is your meaning
illumination, light always beaming,
no surprise, aye no surprise,
that back in Edinburgh,
I enjoyed the gold East Lothian sunrise.

Soldier, Kirkcaldy Soldier

'how you fought your way
through France
for freedoms fight, the chance'

Remembrance Sunday 2016 brought a monumental moment when I had posted my poem of Private Alexander Kennedy titled 'Soldier, Kirkcaldy Soldier' on the 'Old Fife' Facebook page. I was drawn to a comment below from Alex Kennedy;

'My Greatgrandfather Alexander Kennedy was in the Lancashire Fusiliers during WW1, his name is on the memorial in front of the Kirkcaldy library. I had no idea this lovely poem existed. Thank you, I must do research on this.'

SOLDIER, KIRKCALDY SOLDIER ©

Soldier,
Kirkcaldy Soldier
how you fought your way through France
for freedoms fight, the chance
increase the right for peace
to live in peace
Soldier,
Kirkcaldy Soldier

ne'er did you come home
or grow older
Soldier,
Kirkcaldy Soldier
there builds sadness, an inner tear
your bravery, your fear
you Lancashire Fusilier
dearest Soldier
Kirkcaldy Soldier

your name, your stone
from the Great War
and on the Church wall at Abbotshall
proud of you Soldier
Kirkcaldy Soldier

years have passed
were winters colder?
those muddy trenches
Soldier,
Kirkcaldy Soldier
in fields you fought in France
for freedoms fight, the chance
increase the right for peace
rest in peace
courageous Soldier
Kirkcaldy Soldier

Exchanges were made between Alex and myself and it soon became obvious that we both descend from that soldier at rest in France; he went on to add other information;

'My father is Alexander Kennedy as is my Grandfather. Sadly both passed away now. I was led to believe that the Alexander on the memorial was my Great Grandfather. I too have Kirkcaldy connections from time gone by. My Grandfather and father worked on farms in the East Neuk of Fife starting with horses. I haven't looked into this closely but now that I have retired I will have more time to investigate. I'm not 100% sure but I think the Gallatown area features in my family. Thanks for this Robbie, I do wonder if there is some connection. Saying that there are numerous Kennedy families in Fife'

Alex was to answer certain questions regarding the Kennedy's and confirmed with the message below; "These names you mentioned is indeed my family. Thanks again. "

It was actually the names of Alex's grandparents which confirmed that we are on the same Kennedy line.

I couldn't help but think that Alex must've been somewhat unsure or surprised as this stranger knew so much of his family. I was later to send our shared Kennedy / Anderson family tree that I have been working on for many years.

Confidentiality was needed as my dad did not know his Kennedy birth mother therefore Alex and I had to step very carefully. Numerous emails were exchanged and I was fascinated to be reading about people on my Kennedy line.

Alex finding our link to Collessie (dads birthplace) wrote;
'I am a son of Collessie on my mothers side. We are of Scott descendents they stayed in the first thatched cottage as you enter the village at the west end.
I was brought up in Collessie I used to go to the Sunday School. When the beadle retired I was asked if I could ring the church bell every Sunday. I was paid 15 shillings a year. I was 8 or 9 at the time.'

In a later message Alex was to add;
'I have been speaking to my mother, she informed me that my Grandad and Granny who are Scott on her side worked at Halhill Farm 1920. Seems a bit coincidental that my father married a Scott. She did say at that time Grandad Kennedy used to travel about and work at different farms.'

There was another link to St Andrews as Alex himself married Margaret Taylor whose father was a music teacher at Madras College. They have a son named Grant Kennedy who in turn has a son named Brandyn. Grant later married Karen Louden. As you can read the county of Fife; which for almost half a century meant nothing to me; was rapidly growing around me. Soon I was opening up an email of a photo of my great Kennedy uncles and a few days later pictures of a face that I thought that I would never see; my dads birth mother. Questions in a poem of mine that I had given up hope of ever finding was eventually answered.

Poetic Writing of Robbie Kennedy Bennett

She's a Kennedy from Kirkcaldy ©

She worked on a farm in her teenage years
Did she warm to Collessie or cry some tears
Were her clothes so smart or shoddy?
Only her name and not her face
Is all that I had for me to trace
She's a Kennedy from Kirkcaldy.
Yes I only knew her name,
Knowing where she's from but then became
Her blood runs through my body.
And what colour was her eyes and hair?
Deep inside she will be somewhere
She's a Kennedy from Kirkcaldy.

© Robbie Kennedy Bennett
20 May 2006

Pleasantries were passed from then on between our Kirkcaldy and Codsall homes over the festive period and into 2017. March brought something special when one Sunday afternoon Kennedy's for the first time walked into our Bennett family home as Alex and Margaret were on holiday in Ludlow.

Soon we were swapping stories and I got out a file that I keep on dad and Fife. Inside is a page that I have from a magazine that must be over five years old. It is titled 'Charming Collessie, Willie Shand leaves the busier roads of life to explore a Scottish village.' There are three photographs on this page and one being a view of a wee lane that I know well with the church standing proud in the background. It looks to me that Willie Shand the photographer must have taken it from the railway bridge. Another is simply titled 'Thatched cottage.' Surprisingly Alex remarked that it is their old home and in the other the stone building in the wee lane was his great uncles; John Rodger was his name and stayed at Braehead Collessie. This was fascinating to find out and to think that my poem 'Collessie' which mentions thatched cottages was adopted by this beautiful Fife hamlet.

Alex was obviously very interested in finding out more about my dad so I played a cassette tape of him talking in the background in 1982 when Steven had been born. We were all assembled at our house in Beaconsfield Avenue when Lynne and the new baby came home. Alex could tell that his Fife accent had changed somewhat and it had a Wulfrunian twang about it. That was not a surprise as he had left Scotland in the late 1940's to go into the army.

A fortnight later Lynne and I had the pleasure of being in their family home in Kirkcaldy. We also met his mother Jane who was charming to say the least and her knowledge of the Kennedy family was invaluable. Seeing their family photos was amazing and one such picture is of Alex's dad in his kilt and playing bagpipes. He was a member of the Cupar and District Pipe Band which dates back to September 16th 1920. Once again I was stunned as I had liked their page and was following them on Facebook.

Alexander Kennedy, Cupar and District Pipe Band

A Wee Piece
o' th' Heart
Has the Parish of
Dysart

'a scone an' a cup o' tea
out o' the window I stare,
Isabella Kennedy,
has she ever gone past there?'

An anniversary of a sad kind as it is the day that dad died; 31 years to be exact. There's so much that I could tell him such as I have taken Fife to heart. All the villages I have walked through on my coastal path experience. Unearthing addresses of where we once lived. Our Kennedy line; all I found and then finally meeting someone to share it with.

I am looking at old photographs of Dysart Harbour in Fife nearing the end of the 19th Century. Tall masts and ropes of ships give it an interesting olden day maritime feel about the picture. Cargo of coal had either been or about to be filled on the vessels. Severe catastrofic damage to the sea walls happened in 1843. In the photo a building on the left looks remarkably like the Harbourmaster's House, where one hundred and nineteen years later I am looking out of a window at modern day boats moored in the very same harbour.

A Wee Piece o' th' Heart Has the Parish of Dysart ©
Robbie Kennedy Bennett

A Wee Piece o' th' Heart
Has the Parish of Dysart ©

2017

See th' ships a' leaving Dysart Harbour,
in Flesh Wynd whilst a lassie you played,
daughter of a Cooper by trade;
coal and salt exporting history,
ever see a horse drawn cart
along the coast road
heading for the harbour of Dysart?

A scone an' a cup o' tea
out o' the window I stare,
Isabella Kennedy, has she ever gone past there?
my three times great grandmother,
has she ever gone past, gone past there?
Plans were to refresh
in the Harbourmaster's House,
down Hot Pot Wynd a wee gem I find
a restful hour near St Serf's Tower

in the Harbourmaster's House.

A wee piece o' th' heart
has the Parish of Dysart.

In Pathhead I found her address
but the street is less in housing
more so I mean none
disappointingly the house I searched for has gone.
Over the Forth an' further I see Edinburgh
which draws the appreciative eye
rippling sea, gorgeous sky, I could cry.

A wee piece o' th' heart
has the Parish of Dysart.

Isabella Kennedy, you once lived there,
where there is nothing but space
but I see a house and a person, a face.
Isabella Kennedy, it must be you
I'm almost blinded by an easterly view,
in Flesh Wynd, I'd call if this was true
of course not, this is eighteen forty two.
How to hear you talk
go strolling with you down Sailors' Walk,
chatting away from dusk 'till dark

back through the woodlands of Ravenscraig Park,
such a delight, to see castle ruins in a full moonlight;
now summer of eighteen forty three
in the company of Isabella Kennedy.

A wee piece o' th' heart
has the Parish of Dysart.

The Harbourmaster's House
was once Shore House
now the Fife Coast and Countryside Trust
their headquarters and bistro.
They called it 'Little Holland'
those shipowners who sailed in here
into the harbour those ships they steer.
Back in Flesh Wynd in the winter of eighteen forty four
prevent the draught, turn the lock, bolt the door;
the Kennedy household are keeping out
the elements of winter of eighteen forty four.

A wee piece o' th' heart
has the Parish of Dysart.

The lum's a burning
I was in there listening and learning,
came my time to depart

into the Parish of Dysart.
I stepped outside and felt the chilling wind
from the firth blowing on in,
chilling for all of Pathhead
including my Kennedy kin.

A wee piece o' th' heart
has the Parish of Dysart.

You seemed to have spent your life
in this coastal area of Fife,
there I sighed,
a call from heaven aged sixty seven
this greengrocer Dysart woman...
Isabella Kennedy she died.

A wee piece o' th' heart
has the Parish of Dysart.

Summer of two thousand and sixteen
in Dysart Harbour modern boats I had seen,
drifting away as the sun shone in
on a ship called 'Murray and Kennedy kin.'

A wee piece o' th' heart
has the Parish of Dysart.

A scone an' a cup o' tea
out o' the window I stare,
Isabella Kennedy,
has she ever gone past there?
my three times great grandmother,
has she ever gone past, gone past there?

A wee piece o' th' heart
has the Parish of Dysart...

Kinghorn, Look Out For a Wanderer

'lost again in a far away year
Murray, don't you dare disappear'

On the shores opposite from Edinburgh my mind is jigging about like, the 'Raggle Taggle Gypsy O,' song, an upbeat Scottish ballad that's playing out on the Bob Brolly Irish Show this one Sunday afternoon. Any line dancers reading this will surely know the tune as at the time of writing, You Tube shows thousands and thousands of views.

Definitely not my 'raggle taggle' pace as I approached Kinghorn in 2007; not one but two sandy beaches; this wanderer was in awe of what he was seeing. I can recall thinking if this could be picked up and placed on the south coast of England you would never get near to it easily. Years later I found that I have an ancestral connection and it felt good to find out.

I know where I'm from, Rough Hills, Wolverhampton; proud of it, always have been. I wrote a book about it, then another; not forgetting the book about the football team. Maybe so but look some more.

The views were breathtaking, years later, correction as it must have been years before. In fact it was 1821 and the beach looked much the same. There's a lassie walking towards me, she stops in front of me; she smiles because she says that she knows me. Her name is Agnes Orrock Murray and she's been looking out for a wanderer. It's exactly 196 years ago and she's about to get married to Alexander Kennedy. I find earlier family names, are they ours? I turn around and she's gone.

Kinghorn, Look Out For a Wanderer ©

2016

Lost in thought on a Fife coastal road I was on
I looked again in reality and my dream hadn't gone
sunshine was brilliant
radiant on this recipient
Kinghorn was soon to be here
lost again in a far away year
Murray, don't you dare disappear
and you, Mitchell's too, 1700's, nothing new
except on the A921 from Burntisland
there comes a lone wanderer in view.

87

It was closing in on the end of November and Gareth Southgate had been appointed to be the manager of the England football team. Two days later I was to be attending a conference at St George's, home of national football set-up in Burton. Soon to be the festive season and I was thinking if I could get one more visit to Fife before the year's out. Long working hours were draining me and being just over sixty two and a half there was a slight view of retirement. Grandkids were growing, can't believe Aaron the eldest would be ten years old before this school year is out and Liam is not far behind him. Jacob's twenty months and showing his character and Lucas, our new arrival is soon to be a month old. Not forgetting those two bonnie lassies Kiera-Marie and Caitlyn who are all in this bloodline; time was moving on and all had their importance at some time or other and Lynne and I were often called upon. The Scottish ancestral story of ours will fade or grow, who knows? It's down to whatever the next generation decide.

St Andrew's Day 2016 and this man from his generation had just received an afternoon photograph of the Lomond Hills from my new found second cousin. 'Too good to miss,' this gift to me of the Lomond Hills from Alex Kennedy taken at 4pm as he was near Ladybank. Since knowing of each other Alex told me that he can't pass by Ladybank now without thinking of my dad

'The Lomonds, a precious sight
they are to my eyes.'

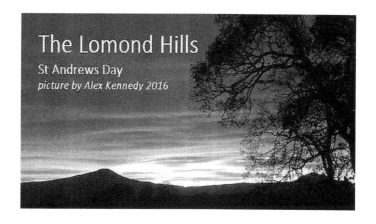

The Lomond Hills
St Andrews Day
picture by Alex Kennedy 2016

One Second of Time
in
The Auld Grey Toun

'as I bow my head,
a feeling of being led
into previous century time'

There are ports and walls around medieval St Andrews but
as far as I know there is no evidence that it was completely
a walled city. It once had several ports into the inner town
but only West Port, at the west end of South Street and the
bottom of The Pends at the harbour entrance remain. Both
these entrances have been renamed since being built. I am
fascinated by these gateways and imagination takes over
whenever they are in view. There is one such arch at the
top end of The Pends; at the east end of South Street; that for
me is completely mind blowing. I have to stoop a wee bit to
get through and just for a second I am transported back to

another age. Amongst many of the famous; royalty included that have ever visited or lived in St Andrews; they most probably done so as well; bowed their head that is. How about if we could cross decades and come face to face with a prince, king or queen or even a fisherman.

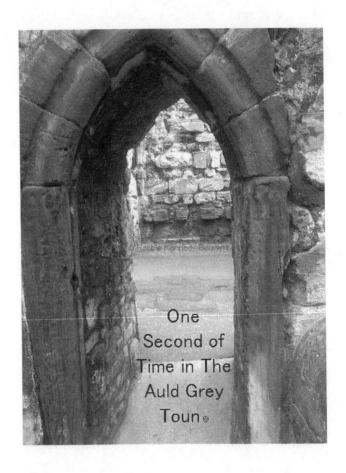

One
Second of
Time in The
Auld Grey
Toun.

One Second of Time
in The Auld Grey Toun ©
2016

All about are reasons for returning
a fire deep inside forever burning,
following my ancestors feet down South Street
into the Middle Ages and through the Pends,
imagination to belong, aye extremely strong
it never ends, nae it never ends.

One at a time, only one at a time
and for one second of that particular time,
as I bow my head, a feeling of being led
into previous century time
for one second of that time.

Bishop Kennedy,
the four Maries with
Mary Queen of Scots,
aye royalty, maids of honour,
St Andreans, pilgrims, every day there's been lots
who have taken their turn, all mine to learn.

But its all about Traill and of Brown
my turn, slightly bowing down,
aye what about them as they all call out
they all call out, they loudly shout
for a second in the archway at St Andrews.

One at a time, only one at a time
and for one second of that particular time,
as I bow my head, a feeling of being led
into previous century time
for one second of that time.

In the auld grey toun, in the auld grey toun,
one second of time in the auld grey toun.

Nine and Five Eighths
of a Mile
From Pittenweem

'on a horse and carriage
and off to see a marriage'

I find it interesting to see road signs with names of villages
and towns in Fife. They are a reminder that I am actually
here. Some are plain and modern and some have an historic
air about them. I can compare it with the feeling of walking
into your grandparents house and seeing ornaments and
fashion of a former time. There appears to be some artistic
designs of later year with the more modern wooden
examples. Hidden in hedgerows are the vintage ones that
our forefathers followed. Fractions of a mile are sometimes
displayed in an artistic way. Once more my research
unearths an interesting fact as Alex Darwood and Paula
Martin have actually written a book 'The Milestones of Fife.'
When finding this on Amazon I could recognise a couple

that they have pictured. One being eye catching at the
island junction of the A917 road out of St Andrews. Taking
the coastal road at that junction there's one more that
informs me that I am nine and five eighths of a mile from
Pittenweem. If it was 1824 then I would be travelling there
to see the marriage of John Duff and Agnes Geddie.

Nine and Five Eighths of a Mile From Pittenweem ©

2016

Here in the year two thousand plus sixteen
a milestone I had seen
on the way to Pittenweem

Red tiled roofs and quaint wee shops
an immediate stop to take it all in,
mate or kin, a vessel may be shared
as they faired the open wave
religion and superstition

the danger of the dark blue sea they brave

There's a lively fish market
early in the harbour at Pittenweem,
coloured crafts and their catch
a merry old match
for the buyer and a price
fish packed in ice will be sold
whilst kept there cold

I've travelled o'er, on land to shore
town to fields and miles of countryside,
biding away back in time
in the agricultural Kingdom of Fife

On a horse and carriage
and off to see a marriage
I'm early and ready
to see a lass named Geddie
as she marries John Duff
at Pittenweem

Nine and five eighths of a mile
from the East Neuk fishing village
called Pittenweem
a milestone I had seen

how keen to get to Pittenweem
to see the red tiled roofs and quaint wee shops
an immediate stop to take it all in
mate or kin, a vessel may be shared
as they faired the open wave
religion and superstition
the danger of the dark blue sea they brave
nine and five eighths of a mile
from the East Neuk fishing village
called Pittenweem

On a horse and carriage
and off to see a marriage
I'm heading on steady
to see a lass named Geddie
as she marries John Duff
at Pittenweem

Now there's red tiled roofs and quaint wee shops
an immediate stop to take it all in....

Still I'm nine and five eighths of a mile
from the East Neuk fishing village
called Pittenweem
here in two thousand plus sixteen

On a horse and carriage
and off to see a marriage
nine and five eighths of a mile
dressed smart and ready
to see a lass named Geddie
as she marries John Duff
at her birthplace Pittenweem
in eighteen hundred plus twenty four

Travelling o'er, on land to shore
town to fields and miles of countryside,
biding away back in time
way back to bygone time
in the agricultural, historical Kingdom of Fife

The Greatest Pleasure
Was Read

'I see it was a lassie that said,
is reconnecting with Scottish roots'

Between those bridges of the Forth and Tay is that county in Scotland that continues to draw my mind. Year on year I find out more and still I keep on searching. I wonder if anyone in my line has ever been to those bridges to see them being built? Did they ever imagine the sight that I can see? Before then my Fife ancestors would've done what all Fifers did and cross on a ferry to either Edinburgh and Dundee.

Many do not find or experience the feeling of where their roots are. If so it is a lost sensation. 'The sun slowly shines over Fife, it cuts through the clouds like a knife.' It certainly cuts through me with serious slices starting at the border.

Back in 2002 my life and existence opened and again in

2012 when first I had grandchildren step into our ancestral kingdom. Then in June 2015 when another journey north contained other great grandchildren of Fife; aye more grandchildren of mine, it was once again a special feeling.

I often think that this writing of mine of ancestral roots will be too early in life for those great grandchildren of Fife. When it is eventually realised I truly hope that it stays with them for their long lifetime.

At home one Sunday in October in my conservatory with a newspaper on my lap. I read something that makes me think that is just how I feel. To connect with Scottish roots is a fantastic feeling no matter where you live your life. In April there is Tartan Day and it's great to see photos on social media of those with Scottish descent in New York showing their tartan. It was an unexplainable proud and somewhat confusing feeling when I first trod on Scottish soil more so when in Fife. I never thought that I would experience anything like it again until grandchildren done so with me. Strange though, the confusing feeling wasn't there.

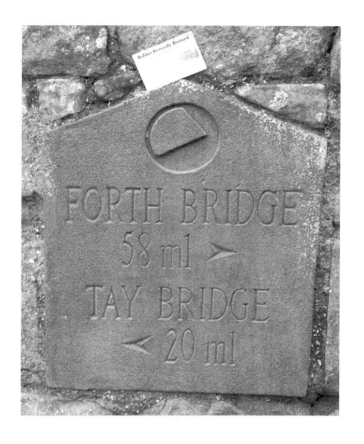

The Greatest Pleasure Was Read ©

2016

The greatest pleasure,was read,
I see it was a lassie that said,
is reconnecting with Scottish roots,
more so when with your children
and loved ones it suits.

I can imagine the stirring of proudness
where ripples and current fight
to see a glimpse of light
in the watching eye,
reflecting the bluest of sky,
and ne'er a tear to cry.

The greatest pleasure,was read,
I see it was a lassie that said,
is reconnecting with Scottish roots,
more so when with your children
and loved ones it suits.

Sun it shone, down on white sand that I walked upon,

a desolate place, feelings race,
heat burned those feelings, I felt ace as they say
in a completely natural way.

The greatest pleasure,was read,
I see it was a lassie that said,
is reconnecting with Scottish roots,
more so when with your children
and loved ones it suits.

To see gold sand is wonderful
enhanced when the sand is nearer to white,
alone in an idyllic setting
I share with my inner self the delight.

White sand, natural green land
a few picturesque stones,
interesting stories have the driftwood
so have the abandoned homes.

The greatest pleasure,was read,
I see it was a lassie that said,
is reconnecting with Scottish roots,
more so when with your children
and loved ones it suits.

There's more to learn outside the classroom
a finding whoever we are,
an acceptance in seeing natural beauty
a finding in the furthest star.

White sand, a kneel down
a feeling that's in your hand,
there's no one for a mile to tell
shout it out, go on you can yell.

There's no music about when needed
no just natural sound,
you find yourself with no one around
senses are surfaced, feelings too
this is you, you feel this is you.

In Edinburgh on a rainy wet Halloween night
thinking back to summer and sunlight,
when grandparents proudly smiled
seeing grandchildren and Scotland reconciled.

The greatest pleasure,was read,
I see it was a lassie that said,
is reconnecting with Scottish roots,
more so when with your children
and loved ones it suits.

Suits you down to a tee
'the origins of this expression are mysterious'
nothing mysterious to me let be said
only a natural feeling
when the greatest pleasure,was read.

Get Tipsy and Tell yer Scottish Tale

'I see a coal fire,
shadows in the room,
shapes on the ceiling
brings on a feeling,
a strange feeling'

It's a winters night in our home on Rough Hills in Wolverhampton. I am just over 3 years old so it must be about 1957. My dad and me are in the back room watching the coal fire burning. I can see shapes and shadows on the walls and ceiling. He says something to me; I don't hear all of the sentence as I was lost in a burning cave; all that I could make out was "Robbie" at the end. Dad was Scotland in those days, I didn't know anything about it then other than kilts and bagpipes.

Sixty years later I am in my Codsall home with a glass of ale in a Scottish beer glass. The handle type that dad used to drink out of. I think about all what I have found out and it could've been let go of quite easily. I've told our family story many times. The auld Scotch songs are heard these days, the meaning eventually broke through. I want to be 3 years old again in front of that coal fire; I've a whole lot of questions to ask.

Bennet

Traill Brown

Anderson

Hunter

Duff Anderson

Kennedy

Get Tipsy and Tell yer Scottish Tale ©

2016

When you're ready Scotland's waiting
waiting in the wings

There's you, look at me,
I'm anything more than three
I see a coal fire, shadows in the room,
shapes on the ceiling
brings on a feeling, a strange feeling.

Something on the television
a word or two in a song, a verse where you may belong.
Surely not wrong to explore, expand perhaps,
tap into a barrel of ancestry ale
yer cannae fail lad, tae get tipsy and tell yer tale.

It hurts deep down thinking that
you could've lived your life never going back,
never going back, back to Scotland.

You could've forgot, a wee bit or the lot,
the very fact that you existed,
but did you do so? most certainly not.

It bothers a stack my conscience gives me flak
"you could've lived your life never going back,
never going back, back to Scotland."

So you pack your case, you may wonder why?
Scotland didnae die, didnae die inside,
it fills yer with pride lad, ay with pride,
yer alive, you get in yer car and drive.

It makes yer bad sometimes, doesn't it lad,
sometimes makes yer sad?
That glad, glad border feeling
shall beat that sadness any day lad
ay beat the sad.

There's you, look at me,
life's moved on, I'm approaching sixty three
I still see that coal fire and shadows in the room,
shapes on the ceiling, they look like wings,
my they look like wings, ay they're wings.

Scotland was waiting, waiting in the wings.

Ay stories stack in that case I pack
how could I have lived my life and never gone back?

never gone back, back to Scotland,

Could've been a thousand experiences lost
into the Tay they could've been tossed,
from the ancestry horses and carriage
go many a birth, death and marriage.

Tap into a barrel of ancestry ale
yer cannae fail lad, tae get tipsy and tell yer tale,
get yourself a plan man
and get yourself off tae Scotland.

Difficult tae Leave
are yer Fife

'awa' an I wasnae prepared
stay, like a fight I was dared'

Aye, it's been said of and described before the difficulty of
this Staffordshire Poet leaving Fife. How remarkable that
these feelings took a hold over me in middle aged life. It's
true that I loved Scotland from a distance and proud to
show it. Then in 2002 the realisation hit me so hard that it
didn't knock me out but opened my eyes.

Driving away from those place names that I can now be
identified with hurts. There is an abandoning feeling; I don't
want to do it but I must as my family are down in England
in my hometown. I cling on to every wee piece of Fife for as
long as I possibly can.

Last year we stopped by and stepped back in time at Culross
and found it charming. The television series Outlander has

been filmed here and understandably so as it has a theme of historical time travelling.

We had parked the car overlooking the Forth; the water was glistening and for anyone listening, I didn't want to leave; I made a promise to keep coming back..

Difficult tae Leave are yer Fife ©

2016

I hung on a wee bit longer
'strung it out' as they say,
as we spent some time in Culross
before heading awa'
awa' on hame o'er the Forth
how come as I cannae believe
Fife, why are yer difficult tae leave?
aye difficult tae leave are yer Fife
awa' an I wasnae prepared
stay, like a fight I was dared
I got out of the car and just stared
and hung on a wee bit longer

An April Day in Collessie, Almost a Hogmanay Tale

'lang you shall for Collessie
to lift the approaching January gloom,
recall that day last April
when daffodils were in bloom'

How the old mind ticks!

I do much the same in my home at Codsall as I do in my ancestral Fife. I love the seasons that the year brings with changing of colour in the landscape. Views of a church always draws my attention and I like to look around the grounds. Codsall has a lovely church and you may have noticed in my posts that it always gets my poetic, photographic mind working.

My dad was born in a farm cottage in the hamlet of Collessie in Fife. That also has a kirk that's a picture within itself. I always try the door whenever there and up until now it has been locked. One day maybe it will be open allowing my mind to explode. On the ground behind the kirk, just like the church of St Nicholas is a countryside view. From Collesie Kirk the farm where my dad was born is quite visible so it holds my imagination.

Over a decade ago I wrote a poem called 'Collessie' and a few years later I was approached by 'Collessie – A Beautiful Village' to display on their website. It was a proud day, still is, now over 90 years since my dad was born there.

It's now over 30 years since we moved to Codsall, my dad died just before we done so. I've got to know many Codsall folk since then and unfortunatly some are at rest at St Nicholas's. I think about them when out early on my early morning Codsall wandering. If you really wish to get into the story google Collessie Kirk and click images.

There's a couple of old Scottish sayings 'noo jist haud on' meaning 'just hold on' and 'whit's fur ye'll no go by ye' which means 'what's meant to happen will happen'

It shall look lovely with the early frosty views approaching Hogmanay and 2017 around St Nicholas Church and 'whit's fur ye'll no go by ye'

'You shall recall one day in April
now the end of the year is in sight,
oh too right you shall, too right'

An April Day in
Collessie,
Almost a
Hogmanay Tale

An April Day in Collessie, Almost a Hogmanay Tale ©

2016

Make the most of the moment appreciably
don't let life pass too easily
too damn fast, make it last lad;
'whit's fur ye'll no go by ye'

You shall recall one day in April
now the end of the year is in sight,
oh too right you shall, too right.

With a festive December mind
that cheery Christmasy head,
moving on o'er to Hogmanay
the season when you're merry and well fed.

Lang you shall for Collessie
to lift the approaching January gloom,
recall that day last April
when daffodils were in bloom.

You shall yearn to walk up that lane again
to the kirk on the wee hill,

wanting to open that door once more
locked, aye it is still;
and you shall think that it's you that's locked out lad;
locked out lad, aye locked out.

You shall again recall that day last April
when the end of this year is in sight,
oh too right you shall, too right.

All you could see was farmland
all you could hear was nowt,
from the ground of the kirk in Collessie
your heart was wanting to shout;
oh too right it was, too right.

But you stayed silent
just you and the love of your life,
you've come a long way from your courting day
in Fife you were with your wife.

You do much the same in Codsall
the lane and Church does draw,
you look on out o'er Staffordshire
and wonder of days of yore.

So I recalled once again that day last April

now the end of this year is in sight,
oh too right, I did too right.

Langing I am for Collessie
to lift the approaching January gloom,
recalling that day last April
when daffodils were in bloom.

Noo jist haud on!

Thinking deep, awake, difficult to sleep;
early year and winter breath;
another anniversary of death
a gift of new life lifts the gloom,
and takes me out of that room
out of the gloom oh ay, out of the gloom oh ay.

Got me going, lying in bed and writing a poem
yearning to do the same, to walk up that lane,
so come swift will ye oh April indeed
Godspeed, oh April Godspeed.

Equally, make the most of the moment appreciably
don't let life pass too easily
too damn fast, make it last lad;
'whit's fur ye'll no go by ye'

Aye jist haud on
it was almost a Hogmanay rhyme
as it lasted beyond Christmas this time,
mindfully and not speedily;
'whit's fur ye'll no go by ye'
oh too right, auld lad, too right.

O John Bennet

'I've searched about The Howff
more than once let me say,
O John Bennet, O John Bennet
I lose myself in the Tay'

The introduction of myself to Alex Kennedy brought great satisfaction and we continued to e-mail each other. A visit to Fife before the festive season 2016 came very close but dropped my plans at the last moment. It was appealing to me that we could have a winter holiday albeit short and a day in Edinburgh to add or my ancestral Dundee.

I have searched hard over the years in finding more about our roots in Dundee. Lynne and I have traipsed the Howff Cemetery many times and I would do some more but I have stretched Lynne's patience to the extreme already. I have found Bennet headstones but as of yet not a link to us.

We have found certain addresses and marriages and much points to hard working class Dundonians. The docks also draw my mind as I stroll about and wonder if I am following in footsteps of my Bennet and Anderson forefathers. John Anderson a boiler maker was present at his daughters wedding in 1868 but unfortunately Jannet Reid his wife was deceased. How sad for 23 year old Jessie, a power loom weaver not to have her mother at her wedding.

The groom was Hector Bennet a ship carpenter, son of John Bennet also deceased; he was a machine fitter. At least his wife Jannet Smith was alive to see their 27 year old son start his new life. Hector and Jessie married in Kings Street which I have found to be refurbished B Listed Georgian townhouses fully restored and modernised.

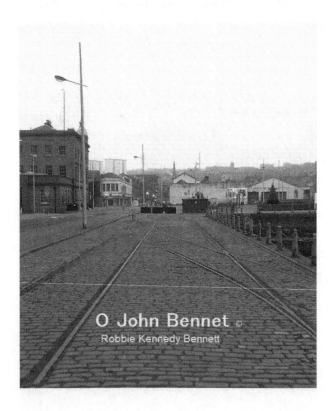

Only a wee tale of New Year Day 2017

O John Bennet ©

2017

No cars back then
sure of that,
about the docks at auld Dundee.
O John Bennet, O John Bennet
whit did become ay thee?

Sir, along Trades Lane,
did you walk down
then after work walk back again?
O John Bennet, O John Bennet
recalling the time I came.

Roots they grew there
in the docks,
through my boots there
and my socks.
flesh and blood, skin and bone
O John Bennet, O John Bennet
here in the docks I stand alone.

Standing, waiting
anticipating that soon
the answer I ask will show,
O John Bennet, O John Bennet
where on earth did you go?

I've searched about The Howff
more than once let me say,
O John Bennet, O John Bennet
I lose myself in the Tay.

In eighteen forty-one
yourself and your son I carry on,
further on down that line,
O John Bennet, O John Bennet
in Dundee I'm trapped in that time.

I'd love to be a laddie
about the docks at Dundee.
O John Bennet, O John Bennet
walking on down with thee.

Please sir, just one morn
on Trades Lane,
to walk down
then walk back again.

O John Bennet, O John Bennet
telling you the time I came.

You'd tell me about
the Smith's, Reid's and Anderson's,
and take me to play with those bairns
on a vibrant Dundee Street,
O John Bennet, O John Bennet
I sure loved the time we did meet.

But there's cars here now
positive of that,
I'd jump at the chance
at the drop of a hat,
if possible there to be
O John Bennet, O John Bennet
with you at the docks in auld Dundee.

O John Bennet, O John Bennet,
whit did become ay thee?

An Ode of a Shiny Fife Pound

'Fife is my future
not only my past
each time I'm there
I want it to last'

Whenever in South Queensferry I look at the Forth Rail Bridge going over to Fife. The views draw something out of me that I never thought existed. How could Scotland be so kind and cruel at the same time?

I grew up a Wulfrunian way and took all what we had in dad for granted not knowing that it would mean so much in later life. At the other side of the Forth in North Queensferry I find that I've built my own past. The photograph taken in 2007 of myself with the rail bridge in the background was chosen for my book 'Wulfrunan Footprints in Fife.'

This coming Spring 2017 will be 10 years since I arrived one early morning in Fife to start walking the coastal path. That chapter in my life has gone too soon but then again so much has happened since. In the story we had become grandparents for the first time and now I can say that four grandchildren have stepped foot in Fife. I truly wish that the others will do so and go there for their bloodline.

This one particular day in my Codsall home I was taking my change out of my trouser pocket and dropped a shiny pound.

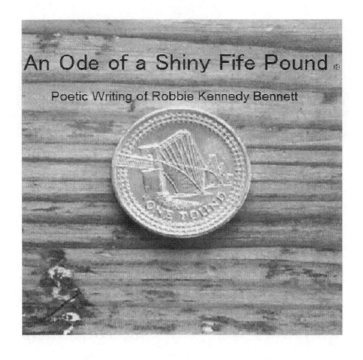

An Ode of a Shiny Fife Pound ©

2016

Here's an ode I found
of a shiny pound
that was a calling me to Fife;

I've been there for my bloodline
aye been there for mine,
I've been there for my bloodline many a time.

Standing, looking, imagining,
feeling, there's definitely a feeling,
a kindred feeling of some sort
when I have brought myself
to be in a particular street
or a particular town
may be a particular position
there I stand and listen
to what Fife is telling
shouting and yelling sometimes
and felling me like a tree
Fife does something to me
Aye there's most definitely something
even when I'm at home.

Then it fell to the ground
did a shiny pound,
tail side up as they say.

It fell on the floor
there before
with that tail side up.

Fife is my future not only my past
each time I'm there I want it to last

to last longer than it does
because I can only describe a belonging
I write these words with a longing
to be back on the road to Fife.

When it fell to the ground
that shiny pound,
tail side up as they say.

It fell on the floor
there before
with that tail side up.

Well I picked it up
that shiny pound
and found that
the reason for falling
must be the calling of Fife.

It was there, I did stare for a second or so
and to the Forth Bridge did I go.

The calling of Fife
came from the falling
of a shiny pound
making not much of a sound

as it landed but...
it was heard in my heart loud and clear
Fife, you're drawing near.

I'll be going there for my bloodline
aye going there for mine,
I'll be going there for my bloodline many a time.

Standing, looking, imagining...

Climbing Down a Ladder of Past Time in Old Dundee

'did they watch outside these gates?
meaning those from who I descend'

"You're almost a Fifer" I was once told. Another person said "so, you're a Dundonian." Both being said by people who could tell by my writing that I have feelings for this eastern area of Scotland. Not only my writing but the physical challenges that I have taken on. The coastal path and the Lomond Hills are never far away from my thoughts. Then in 2016 when I got something out of my system and made my way to the top of the Law that overlooks Dundee. The summit is quite visible from the north area of Fife and was simply a 'must do' for me.

I had climbed the Law before breakfast on this pleasant day in 2016. A feeling difficult to explain when looking down on the Tay and Dundee which holds much of my ancestry.

138

It was just about dawn and I caught a spectacular sunrise
which is most probably a common occurrence for these
Dundonians. I could see the docks and thought of my ggg
grandfather whose trade was there. Later that morning
Lynne and I would be taking in the shops and before lunch
looking about the church grounds of one of the spires of
Dundee that I was looking down on.

Climbing Down a Ladder of Past Time
in Old Dundee © Robbie Kennedy Bennett

Climbing Down a Ladder of Past Time in Old Dundee ©

2017

Did they worship here I wonder?
meaning those in my family tree
they lived only yards away
from St Andrew's Parish Church
aye only yards away in Dundee.

I've gone up that path, tried the door
down that path and up once more,
I've read every name on a headstone
aye every single one,
of someones loved ones gone.

Shaped dwarf conifers are they?
steps, my shoes have climbed,
then quite suddenly momentarily I'm
climbing down a ladder of past time.

Did they talk outside these gates?
meaning those whose blood I share,
they lived only yards away
aye only yards away back there.

140

I bet they were lad, those Dundonians
who attracted me here,
they distracted me from all that I do
and towards this church I steer.

How many tears in so many years?
have dried on a cotton handkerchief,
in a glove or a ladies sleeve
in disbelief and good reason to grieve.

Did they watch outside these gates?
meaning those from who I descend,
they lived only yards away
I stand by these gates and pretend.

Aye, pretend, pretend to be with them
when a bride and groom come towards
and the bride looked beautiful
the groom smiled at one of us here
who lived only yards away
so he must be known
possibly lived somewhere near.

Ten minutes to noon the clock does say
soon this laddie is to be walking away,

from St Andrew's Parish Church
on this pleasant Dundee day.

Did they walk away I wonder?
meaning those in my family tree
they lived only yards away
from St Andrew's Parish Church
aye only yards away in Dundee.

Did they worship there I wonder?
climbing down a ladder of past time again,
wondering about my ancestors
up St Andrews Street they came.

Church of Scotland
Sunday Service 11am
All Welcome

Did they worship there I wonder;
I can't help but wonder?

Children of the Fisherfolk

'they're playing in North Street
are the children of the fisherfolk,
women with aprons
and skirts ankle length
motherly female strength'

North Street and surrounding streets in St Andrews always draws my attention whenever there or in photograph. This being as we have some addresses of ancestral residence. This part of town was once known as the fisher quarter and housed the fisher families. Fishermen and their wives worked in the streets mending nets in preparation for the next stint out at sea. Many of the old photographs are taken outside a certain few houses in North Street.

On one particular picture the view is looking along to St Salvator's and looks very similar today. A few dwellings have been demolished but the imaginative mind can see

former times. Mothers are looking at the photographer
almost suspiciously whilst children play.

My modern day photograph taken by myself is from the
other side of the road. I picture the lassies there in 1910
happily playing with their skipping rope and that child
dancing in the road and of course those fisher women
looking at that photographer. I know they are as I am
watching it all happen!

Children of the Fisherfolk
Robert Kenneth Bennett

Children of the Fisher Folk ©

2017

They're playing in North Street
are the children of the fisher folk,
bairns in mothers arms
lassies with a skipping rope,
too innocent and early
for young ladies charms.

Another child is happily dancing
prancing around in the road,
no vehicles on North Street then

in nineteen hundred and ten.

Many a cracked pavement slab
weather looks drab,
in the fisher quarter they play
a few eyes on the photographer this day.

They're playing in North Street
are the children of the fisher folk,
women with aprons and skirts ankle length
motherly female strength.

I studiously stare at one dwelling
a glimpse of an open pillared forestair,
nobody looking at this photograph
cares as much to be looking as closely there.

They're playing in North Street
are the children of the fisher folk,
wearing winter clothes
the children of those fisher folk.

North Street lanterns yet alight
waiting for the blackness of the night,
glowing, flickering in the dark
then hark at the North Sea hark!

Children of the fisher folk sleep
in rooms and beds they share,
after songs and candlelight reading
then goodnight after a fisher folk prayer.

Storms come often I imagine
gales blow this time of the year,
into the heart of St Andrews
near to the Little Cross here.

I close my eyes and hear the night
wind does howl, sometimes roar,
blowing 'reit up' North Castle Street
cliff-top ruins, there's a dangerous shore.

They're playing in North Street
are the children of the fisher folk,
College Chapel, St Salvador's I can name
somehow the street looks the same.

Without the children of the fisher folk,
playing in the picture contentedly,
as fathers of the fisher children
are fishing out at sea.

They're playing in North Street
are the children of the fisher folk,
a long gone St Andrews view
children of the hard living fisher folk
swing that rope, dance that dance
in that realistic photograph
you've go me skipping into.

You Came Back

'you must feel it's purposeful
that it's worthwhile,
when you leave you go out in style?
In reality we know that you don't
we can tell by a mile'

The people and the land call me back time after time and year after year. I haven't tired of or taken for granted the feeling of arriving in Fife. The joy is real, experiences are memorable; should've done it earlier in life.

I study a map of Fife with familiarity of the towns and villages. From Dunfermline to Dysart those Hunter, Rae and Kennedy ancestors know that I am here. The Anderson and Duff kin also see that their blood has crossed over the Forth. Bennet, Traill and Brown hear news that I have arrived in the kingdom. Church bells in St Andrews ring out in celebration; no they don't, in reality nobody knows except me and my imagination.

You Came Back ©

2017

I see you came back
we thought that you would,
we've a strong call haven't we?
that makes you feel good;
I see you came back.

You must feel it's purposeful
that it's worthwhile,
when you leave you go out in style?

In reality we know that you don't
we can tell by a mile.

You're quiet when you arrive
and wonder who you really are
e'en though you're alive;
to your love who knows you well
she understands
there's no reason to tell.

Confused, two localities are fused,
together in your being
seeing all that you see
and all about us, all about we.

Collessie is peaceful
deep in thought you stand,
feeling all the ingredients of
this agricultural land.

Well, you came back
we thought that you would,
we've a strong call haven't we?
that makes you feel good;
you came back.

We can tell by a mile
how do we know?
It shows in your eyes
in your tearful eyes as you go, as you depart
the sadness in your heart:
we feel it too, we don't like losing and
especially you.

Good, you came back
we thought that you would,
we've a strong call haven't we?
that makes you feel good;
you came back.

We don't want to lose you,
pleased you came back...

Everlasting Sleep in Fife Ground

'and I shall continue to do so
as long as my time does allow
'cause I'm used to it now'

There's a joy and sadness combined whenever finding a place of final rest. You stare, read the words and a feeling surfaces. You're more knowledgable of your own being; the thought that you knew yourself and realise you didn't. From then on you are connected more so to that person and exact locality. No matter how long ago that they have passed on there is still a somber feeling. There's silence, there's noise; you listen and look around. You get used to the feeling but still there's an air of responsibility to return again.

154

Everlasting Sleep in Fife Ground ©

2017

I'm used to it now
as I've been calling
for a few years.
I shed no tears
as it's a case of finding
and not knowing;
nevertheless when going
I always happen to
stand and read a name
the simple reason I came;
and I shall continue to do
as long as my time does allow
and I'm used to it now.

When I say not knowing
it's meant in a way
of not being in their company,
not hearing them talking
and seeing them walking
into a room, living long
or leaving too soon;
still I imagine, picture,

being around
instead of everlasting sleep
in Fife ground; to keep me calling
as long as my time does allow
and I'm used to it now.

When I say that
I've not shed a tear
doesn't mean I don't care
for I always get there
as you well know
and I shall continue to do so
as long as my time does allow
'cause I'm used to it now.

I'm used to it now
the cemeterial sound
of Fife ground;
I'm used to it now.

Driving Away From Tayport

'just being there lighted
something deep, can only
describe what you dream about
in your sleep and wonder why?'

Those who know me well will connect me to sport; especially football. Our family home on Rough Hills, Wolverhampton was only a two hundred sprint away from Dixon Street playing fields. Countless hours of mine was spent on that field playing football. At the most there was three pitches with two of them disappearing but one remained and is still in use today. I often drive by and can recall my very first game on there for All Saints Junior School. This would be in 1963 when I was nine years old. There's an amusing poem of mine titled 'Bennett You're Offside' which in fact is a true story as I didn't understand the rule and that's what was being shouted to me.

157

'I thought that I was in heaven,
When he gave me shirt number seven.
Nothing that day could dent my pride,
They called me Bennett You're Offside'

Many seasons have rolled on by since those childhood, youthful, enjoyable days and still the power of football controls me. I played on many football pitches and non-league grounds around the midlands and beyond; picking up many injuries along the way. I also made friends and for all I know enemies as I did compete greatly, that Scottish blood in me, and scored plenty of goals.

The marathon boom was all the craze in the 1980's and certainly took me on a fabulous journey for a few years. On the eve of this one Wolverhampton Marathon I was registering at the Civic Centre in town. There was stalls on show with vests, running shoes etcetera and a pair of shorts drew my attention. They were blue with the rampant lion of Scotland on. "They'll do for me," and I proudly wore them in many races. I was totally wrapped up in sport during my twenties and thirties and regrettably did not think beyond my immediate family boundaries. My wishful poem 'I Should've Played for Ladybank Violet' says it all really. It mentions that I should've gone to Fife in my sporting prime but unfortunately did not do so. I did though try to make amends in 2007 with my first stretch of walking the Fife Coastal Path from North Queensferry to Leven. In 2008 the coastal walk was completed when I walked into Dundee. Many games of football and races have been forgotten but I can't see this adventure fading away.

> *'I should have played*
> *for Ladybank Violet,*
> *a scout may have seen me*
> *and signed for Dundee.*
> *I could have been*
> *capped for Scotland,*
> *that's what I*
> *would have chosen for me'*

One Summer evening driving away from the Tayport v St Andrews Juniors United fixture brought great satisfaction that I was here as a spectator but tinged with that regrettable feeling. Aye, it would have been great to have seen my name on that teamsheet.

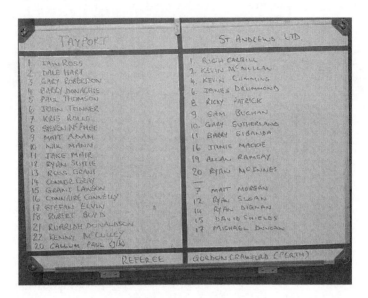

Driving Away From Tayport ©

2017

I recall the sun was low,
blinding at times even
near the starting of the 2013–14 season
that shall last for months and months.

This game didn't have a sell out capacity
but a noticeable semi-professional tenacity,
the level was high in fact
and Tayport Football Club to be exact.

Aye, Tayport were playing
St Andrews Juniors United,
just being there lighted
something deep, can only
describe what you dream about
in your sleep and wonder why?
Why oh why did I dream about that.
There you go, that's the state of mind I am at.

I have a connection to Tayport
and as you know St Andrews,
so let's fuse them here an now
a good, good reason to go:
aye to watch this game, it wasnae tame yer see
no, says me, there was a spark of electricity.

Afterwards I drove home, well not exactly
but to a caravan in St Andrews.
I'm known for loving football
but not in a million years
would the auld man have thought

that one day I would be here
listening to a hundred or so of Fifers' cheer.

It was the same but different feeling
a mixture of the two, aye who would've
thought you'd be driving away from
a game in Tayport?
How about that Jock, how about that!

Well, as I've told; I recall the sun was low,
blinding at times even
near the starting of the 2013-14 season
that shall last for months and months.

There shall be bitter winds that blow
sleet and deep, deep snow,
forcing cancellation and frustration
to many members there,
where the Tay is only a wee walk away.

Countless games I have departed
got into my car and started
the short or long journey away
but never this close to the Tay.

I stand here alone on land I can claim as my own,

well, that's a bit of an exaggeration
and an explanation I need and proud indeed
of my roots Bennet, Kennedy, and Traill,
and the Mighty River Tay
this happy wanderer does sail.

So there's the reason to be a spectator
no commentator gave me
a loudspeaker announcement;
just me, looking, listening,
watching a game but;
the strangest of all was the feeling
and that I can't explain.

I shall leave it as; I recall the sun was low,
blinding at times even
near the starting of the 2013-14 season
that shall last for months and months.

That being the drive back home to St Andrews
through Leuchars and o'er the Eden at Guardbridge;
emotional but not nearing a state of tears,
the strangest of all was the feeling
that shall last for years and years.

Marie's Wedding

Mairi's Wedding (also known as Marie's Wedding, the Lewis Bridal Song, or Mairi Bhan) is a Scottish folk song originally written in Gaelic. The song is on my mind because in May 2017 our daughter Marie is getting married. There's been plenty of preparation going on for a while now for her marriage to Mark and suddenly the date is in sight. And another welcome addition is that Madison officially becomes a step-granddaughter.

Kisses and Wishes and Then I've Scared Away the Bogeymen

'what do you do with Daddy?
when his little girl has grown
a father child relationship
is a special one to own'

I needed to find something that connected my dad to Marie
but I was finding it difficult. She reminded me that Kiera-
Marie was born on what would be his birthday. That in
itself is special to me every year the date comes around. I
had a poem that I wanted to use (wrote with Marie in mind
and 'borrowed' by a friend); a father to daughter on her
wedding day and wanted to add something else. Her
grandad Jock had passed on in 1986 therefore she would be
very young and little brother Steven more so. This one
Saturday afternoon not long after the new pound coin
release in March 2017; we found her Coin Album with her
collection from when she was a schoolgirl. It immediately
got Lynne's and my attention as we were reminded of what
she had in the album. Suddenly as if it was meant to be I
noticed a £2 coin with a thistle and above was the year
1986.

Kisses and Wishes and Then
I've Scared Away the Bogeymen ©
2011

Once upon a time
in these strong masculine arms of mine
I held a bundle of a baby girl
more precious than a priceless pearl
in her Daddy's world

What do you do when you are dad?
and she's frightened or she's sad
She deserved my utmost best
my instinct done the rest

How can you measure the treasure of a daughter?
Is she the only treasure we have pleasure of giving away?
Setting off to sail in the deep, deep water
sailing on a ship called 'Love' upon her wedding day

What do you do with Daddy?
when his little girl has grown
A father child relationship
is a special one to own

****

Her pretty little hand
once held mine so tight
Her pretty little face
I kissed and wished goodnight sleep tight

Kisses and wishes and then
I've scared away the bogeymen
Why? because I'm daddy
keeping away the baddie

These are the arms she ran to
This is the man that's stronger than
Batman, Robin and Superman

These are the arms she wrestled
This is the chest where she nestled when I carried
This is the hand that gave her away when she married

What do you do with Daddy?
When his daughters a beautiful bride
catching all her compliments
inside he's bursting with pride

How can you measure the treasure of a daughter?
I've learned a Father's way
it is on her wedding day

****

What do you do with Daddy after his speech?
There's his heart and there's his hand
That's always there to reach.

Anderson,
Stand Sure Anderson

'an oak, proper and strong
some wee splinter in that oak
you can say that I belong'

Our eldest grandaughter Kiera–Marie was waving at me
from the bedroom window early one Saturday morning as I
stepped out of our house to walk up to Codsall village.
Remarkably at the time I was going over the verses of my
poem about Anderson female ancestors. Both Kiera and
elder brother Liam had had a sleep over at their nanny
Lynne and grandad Robbies'. Little did I know at the time
that it would run into a Saturday night as well.

This also led into an interesting morning as grandson Liam
was with me for the day and we were on our way to see a
Saturday morning game of football. We were driving by
Bushbury Crematorium and I decided to stop and show him
where his great grandad Jock's ashes were laid. When in the

car and picking up our journey he wanted a song played that we did when driving home over the Forth Road Bridge in June 2016. 'Will Ye No Come Back Again' was soon to be heard in a vehicle approaching Wednesfield.

Anderson, Stand Sure Anderson ©
Robbie Kennedy Bennett

Anderson, Stand Sure Anderson ©

2017

Anderson, I wish to acknowledge
the name of Anderson.
Stand Sure, Anderson
there upon your crest
that badge that some proudly
wear on a hat on their head
or shirt on their breast;
Anderson, with an oak tree also,
an oak, proper and strong
some wee splinter in that oak
you can say that I belong.

Two sides of the Scottish side of me

there's Anderson,
aye, there's twice Anderson.

There's Jessie from Dundee
daughter of John, a ship fitter,
and there's a family line that goes on
carries on into Angus.

She married in 1868
in Dundee when jute weaving was high,
tall chimneys bellowed smoke
into the Dundee sky.

Then there's a daughter of Peter
a ploughman from Kingsbarns,
St Andrews is nearby
nearby, a good reason to cry
when I'm in Kingsbarns.

Oh I could cry for Agnes
she was too young to leave,
her husband and their bairns
sad circumstances I believe.

Anderson, I wish to acknowledge
the name of Anderson.

Stand Sure, Anderson
there upon your crest
that badge that some proudly
wear on a hat on their head
or shirt on their breast;
Anderson, with an oak tree also,
an oak, proper and strong
some wee splinter in that oak
you can say that I belong.

Jessie she married into Bennet
Kennedy, Agnes she wed,
in the research I found
and the information that I read;
those Anderson lassies.

Anderson, son of Andrew
your kinship is deep in me
and the patron St Andrew
is with me at the sea
aye, at my adorable St Andrews.

Kilrymont, the 4th century;
legend has it; St Regulus by sea he came
shipwrecked, with the relics of St Andrew
and there did change the name

from Kilrymont to St Andrews.

Jessie daughter of John, Agnes of Peter,
find me a stage, fill me a theatre,
Anderson tartan, modern, ancient or dress,
wrap them around me for Jessie and Agnes
your names I caress, you're pure,
stand sure, Anderson stand sure.

Anderson, I've acknowledged
the name of Anderson.
Stand Sure, Anderson
there upon your crest
that badge that some proudly
wear on a hat on their head
or shirt on their breast;
Anderson, with an oak tree also,
an oak, proper and strong
some wee splinter in that oak
you can say that I belong.

Let me hum an auld scotch song for Anderson
aye, those lassies I call mine named Anderson.

Do Yer Nae
Wanae Leave K'cody?

'what do yer feel Rab,
what do yer see?'

It was nearing Spring 2017 and there was a calling inside of me to make plans to have our first break of the year in Fife. Lynne had to take her holidays by a certain time which tied into another ancestral event. The winter had been hard going with us engaging in grandparent availability. For myself it was getting Aaron and Caitlyn to school on a Tuesday and Wednesday with Lynne picking them up on a Monday and Tuesday afternoon. More often than not there is a CD in my car relevant to Scotland which I can play at the press of a button. These two mornings I have the radio set on Heart FM or something similar as I had noticed that they sing along to certain songs.

This week approaching our Fife journey was an eventful one family wise. We were to be away for Mothers Day so

176

my mom had came over the Sunday before and we surprised her with a card and flowers. Aaron had been selected for the school football team on Tuesday in which it was pleasing to see him play well and score a smashing goal. It was Kiera-Marie's birthday on Thursday, sharing with my dad, and I had joined our daughter Marie in meeting her out of school. That was a good experience as Jacob aged 2 had walked all the way there with us. From there it was a drive over to Brewood to watch Liam run in a cross country running event. The day wasn't finished there as Aaron had to be picked up in Perton to take him to football coaching where Steven his dad met us at the Aldersley dome. Yes an eventful day which started with me picking up Teri, Stevens partner, and 5 month old and youngest grandchild Lucas and take them to the club shop at Molineux. It was here that the chance could not be missed by having our picture taken by the Stan Cullis statue. He doesn't realise it yet that 'like his grandad before him he's gold.' I wonder who has wrote a poem about that?

It wasn't to stop there as Liam was to be attending soccer coaching late Friday afternoon so the grandad duties were stretched to the limit. Saturday was fast approaching and the early start to Fife was getting closer. It was also Aaron's 10th birthday and all had been arranged; gift, card and when to call. So the drive to Scotland and interestingly his birthday coincides with the day that Robert the Bruce became King!

Approaching 5.00am on our Codsall drive I am spraying de-icer on the car windscreen and six hours later we are basking in the sun on Kirkcaldy seafront overlooking the Forth.

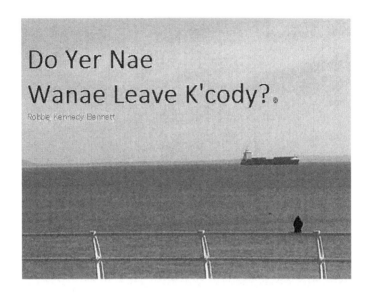

Do Yer Nae Wanae Leave K'cody? ©

2017

Keep looking whilst yer here,
don't yer leave now and disappear,
when yer look out at sea
what do yer feel Rab, what do yer see?
like that bird Rab, do yer nae wanae go
do yer nae wanae leave K'cody, Rab,
do yer nae wanae go?

Come to Shorehead

'laddie, have you come to see the dawn?
the appearance of first light,
did you sleep well last night?
high on the Kinkell Braes'

We called Aaron from Kirkcaldy and wished him happy birthday and let him tell us what his gifts were. My mind went back to when he was born and I had first stepped out on my Fife Coastal Path walk in May 2007; we had become grandparents for the first time.

'welcome to the world bairn Aaron,
joy into lives he'll bring,
born on a day when
Robert the Bruce became King'

The cross country road to our destination was quite picturesque and the day was turning out to be the best of the year so far. Suddenly St Andrews Bay came into to view with what we agreed was a sea of beautiful blue. It was almost in disbelief that if my research is correct that ancestors of ours were owners of fishing yawls when in 1803 when there was just three. Later that evening Lynne and I were in the Whey Pat public house opposite West Port and old photographs on the wall drew my attention as I searched for a family name.

'On Saturday 25th March 2017 at 8.30pm, thousands of people from across Scotland will join millions around the world in turning off their lights for one hour in a huge, symbolic show of support for action on climate change, and for a more sustainable future.'

On the Sunday morning it was ridiculously quiet on the St Andrews to Anstruther road as I was walking that way back to our caravan. I could not help but imagine that this is how it would've sounded a century back. All that I heard was my boots on the gravel path, gulls near the coast to my left and on my right birds in the woods; if I were an expert I'd tell you exactly what type they were but I'm afraid that I'm not. Suddenly there was the sound of horses hooves as two

riders came over the hill and down the coast road.
Disappointingly modern age took over as the higher I got
on the hill more traffic appeared and the calm of previous
time was interrupted. Many thoughts crossed my mind
when walking that coastal road, such as Traill and Brown
on my Bennet side or Anderson and Duff on my Kennedy's.
Well why not as this was the road back and forth to the old
grey toun from Kingsbarns and beyond. Crop from the
fields and fish from the sea would have needed
transporting.

The weather forecast for today was to be sunny and breezy
but fortunately the wind was hardly noticeable. My
Wolverhampton cousin Paul and Jacqui his partner were to
spend time with us and we had a pleasant drive to Loch
Leven. Mary Queen of Scots was imprisoned in the island
castle and forced to abdicate the crown. It was still March
but midges were in their plenty and found Lynne's cream
coat attractive. I was drawn to the water of the loch being a
lovely colour of blue. Then to the overlooking West Lomond
which this happy wanderer has climbed. Suddenly it is the
evening of the 2nd May 1568 and festivities had been
taking place. Is that Jane Kennedy I see, a maid of hers
helping to break free from confinement? She must have
been close as Mary chose her along with another to help
her on to the scaffold for her execution in 1587; apparently

Jane Kennedy was her lady in waiting that tied her blindfold. Unlike Mary Queen of Scots at Lochleven there was no escaping for me; from a viewing point in Perth and Kinrosshire I knew that my heart was held captive in Fife.

"Look at that sky" said Paul later back on Kinkell Braes. It was an amazing colour of red with feint streaks of blue and I doubt if an artist could've caught it in paint. Not in all my years have I ever seen such a sky and soon other people were outside taking photographs. I looked down on my ancestral St Andrews at another stunning view with a feeling of pride and thanks of where my roots are. Paul again said something that struck a chord in me, "who'd a thought old chap that you and I would've met up here? "I know" I replied, "if we had both stayed in Wolverhampton we may not have met again. So there beneath the red sky on the Kinkell Braes, two grandsons of Benjamin James Owen and Sarah Ann Williams, both from All Saints in Wolverhampton, toasted ourself; well he did as was the only one who had a drink! Amusing it was and fortunately Jacqui caught it on video.

It is nearing 4.00am in a dark caravan bedroom as I write this paragraph when I realise that the red sky has had an affect on me before. That was three years ago when my maternal grandmother Sarah Ann, having not had one

Summer with her, she came into my thoughts one Sunday red sky late afternoon; has she done it again this time with another grandson?

> *"my fifty ninth Summer*
> *if true Sarah Ann if true,*
> *then I've spent this Summer with you."*

Come to Shorehead ©

2017

Laddie, have you come to see the dawn?
the appearance of first light,
did you sleep well last night?
high on the Kinkell Braes.

Yesterday, a sunshine of a welcome
enjoyment down on the sands,
a right good summertime feeling,
peeling on back wintertime clothes;
many folk out on a stroll,
a whole new outlook for all;
except for you, there's a call;
an unexplainable call.

Come ye back once more
to see the Bonnie old shore,
come be where Isabella was born
come see the dawn, the amazing dawn;
your kin, they were a witness and in you it's within.

186

Laddie, far away laddie,
have you come to see the dawn?
be where your great grandmother was born,
come to Shorehead by the braes and the shores
and rest awhile laddie,
here you should ponder and pause
for a few moments auld laddie,
what you see is all yours.

Relics an' th' Ruins

'sae peaceful, sae calm,
nae harm yer are a doin'

Modern day pilgrims travel from all over the world to come
to St Andrews. You see them wandering about the cathedral
ruins taking photographs. It doesn't need much imagination
to see that it would have been an impressive building, it
amazes me how men of that day could build something of
that size without the aid of machinery. The cathedral was
Roman Catholic and built in 1158 taking over a 100 years
to complete. It doesn't need a mathematician to work it out
that the men who started it didn't complete it.

The Scottish Reformation of the 16th century divided
people; this being when the church and religion was a part
of everyday life. Eventually Catholicism was outlawed and
religious buildings fell into disuse. There was soon
abandonment of this once magnificent structure and it fell
into a ruinous state. Apparently there was no preservation
until 1826.

In 2008 when walking the coastal path the sight of the ruins was pleasing to see. They fit well into the first sight of St Andrews and pilgrims of the past taking this route I imagine would be joyful. What wasn't known by myself at the time is that there is final resting places of my ancestors in the grounds of the cathedral ruins; once finding it was not to be forgotten. This amongst other names that have been discovered in Scotland cemented my belonging. You need to imagine that at the time I was a middle aged man from Wolverhampton and had not really given it thought. I am not being disloyal in any way to my Wulfrunian ancestry, in which I am extremely proud of; but it was like being in a room and the light is switched on. I saw so much of who I am and there's probably more to find.

Most often I am wandering far too early in St Andrews and the cathedral gates are not yet open for the day. Believe me, later people shall come and in their plenty. From the cliff I can pick a stone out and I have done so from someones photograph taken at the top of St Rule's tower which is a 100ft or 33m high. I peer through the gate from the cliff to see if I can catch a glimpse of the almost square headstone with a wavy top edge. Later I try the gate at this end of North Street by the war memorial and it's still locked.

Aye, but when I can I stand before; and proud to say that
my son and 4 grandchildren have done so; James Trail, a
Baker of St Andrews who died in 1806 aged 43 years; at
rest in the cathedral grounds amongst the relics and the
ruins.

Relics an' th' Ruins ©

2017

Sae peaceful, sae calm,
nae harm yer are a doin
as yer wonder 'bout the relics
an' th' ruins o St Andreas;
St Rule's Tower
less mysterious at this hour;
less sae, less sae.

Saltire, Hardly Blowin'

'down to the ruins I'm goin'
for an hour perhaps two
as I take in view after view'

I write these words early upon Kinkell Braes with hardly a breeze, listening to the waves tumbling onto the East Sands as the sea is stimulating the old mind. Cloudy grey is the sky and may well be for the rest of the day. At the bottom of the path I pause and write again. I think of the shipwrecks that have happened in looking distance of where I am. I see my ancestors out there fishing for their living and to feed a family. It's now 7.05am, all done and finished; the saltire flag is hardly blowing; I best get going to the toun, the auld grey toun.

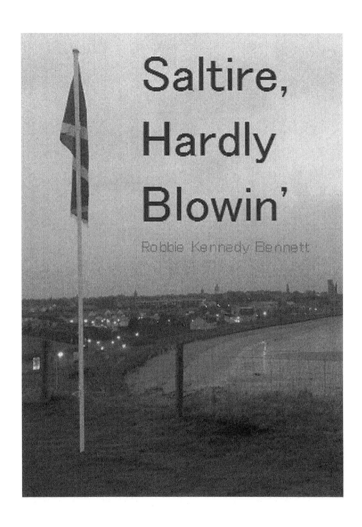

Saltire,
Hardly
Blowin'

Robbie Kennedy Bennett

Saltire, Hardly Blowin' ©

2017

Stepping out, eyes on the bay this grey day
lighter in colour than the toun
only just, aye it's a must
to get down to the auld grey toun.

Saltire, hardly blowin'
down to the ruins I'm goin'
for an hour perhaps two
as I take in view after view.

Saltire, aye hardly blowin'
year on year I'm knowin'
thoughts they are a flowin'
around the bay.

Waves, they're a rollin'
here I am a stoppin' an strollin'
come what may.

Saltire, hardly blowin'
in the North Sea I'm a rowin'

with a strong arm and sturdy oar
to disembark on old Kilrymont shore.

Stepping down, eyes on toun, eyes on the toun.

Anywhere
and Everywhere
in St Andrews

*'you clear my head
then fill it full of imagination'*

Aye the saltire was hardly blowing and soon I was on the
cliff edge peering through the cathedral gates that won't be
open for at least two hours. From the cliff path I can just
make out the gravestone that is in my Trail ancestry line
dated 1806. What's amazing is that two scores years ago I
didn't know of any such link to St Andrews.

Out in North Street from Gregory Place I had to carefully
cross the road as it can be busy on this corner. Back across
the street in between vehicles I imagined the fisherfolk

tending their nets and the fisher children playing. How times change as one after another vehicles drove in between my vision. Down South Castle Street, shame that the building is no more where my folk resided over 90 years ago. Turning the corner and making my way to the Pends I was drawn into the year of 1564. It was horse drawn travel only as Mary Queen of Scots came out of the house where she stayed on South Street.

She glanced at me then her maids guided her back into the building and closed the door behind her.

Anywhere and Everywhere in St Andrews

Anywhere and Everywhere
in St Andrews ©

2017

You clear my head
then fill it full of imagination,
I see an old photograph
and wonder if that's a relation?
standing there, aye anywhere in S Andrews.

Tide rolls in and out
sometimes whispers or does shout
all depending on the weather
hand in hand they go together.

The sun, rain, wind and sea
brings all different thoughts from me
I grow like the tallest tree
then shrink so dramatically

Only another bystander
who gets caught in a new photograph,
"look at him there," aye anywhere,
anywhere in St Andrews.

Just clearing my head

filling it full of imagination,
from the harbour to the old station
old photographs, do I see a relation?
standing there, aye everywhere in S Andrews.

This rhyme ends, coming down The Pends,
aye, it's all been said, I was just clearing my head,
but all is silent, still I imagine, pretend,
hush now...., hush now, hush now,
this rhyme ends, coming down The Pends.

William Wallace

'he began the revolt in Lanark
In the spring of twelve ninety seven,
he routed a large English army
at Stirling on September eleven'

There is a road in Fife that always makes me feel as if I want
to know more about. In fact it's more than one road as it
crosses the A92 and eventually leads to the M90. The road
is actually the one that goes from Cupar towards Perth.
Looking at my map it is the A913 and goes by or may be in
the small parish of Moonzie, then Dunbog, Abdie and
Newburgh; apologies if I have missed any out. It's really
rural to a lad that was born and raised on a
Wolverhampton council estate and enforces the love of
countryside out of me. Dunbog Primary School built in
1839 still contains a feel of how life was for Fifers in those
days and into the turn of the 20th Century. The school
always attracts my attention and takes me into the
childhood of another. Ruins, such as Collairnie Castle and
Abdie church nearing Lindores gives an imaginary feeling

of the history that these roads must have. Suddenly I see
clansmen following who I presume to be William Wallace;
victorious from the battle of Black Irnsyde.

William Wallace

Of

Elerslie

1272AD-1305AD

BRAVEHEART

With confidence Edward left Scotland
This land he thought he'd secured,
Scots detested his arrogant regime
Their challenge he then soon endured.

William Wallace an Ayrshire landowners son
Inspired others to rise and fight on,
His passion for vengeance
Was mighty and strong
The people of Scotland soon fought along.

He began the revolt in Lanark
In the spring of twelve ninety seven,

He routed a large English army
At Stirling on September eleven.

Wallace ruled Scotland for no more than a year
Defeated at Falkirk and Stirling was near,
Since 1298 England's armoury did fail,
But then came a day in 1304
Stirling Castle was Edwards once more.

William Wallace still influenced affairs
The English held Sterling
But it would never be theirs.
So then he was captured alive
Executed at Smithfield in 1305.
In shackles and chains
Convicted of high treason,
A threat to proud Edward
Or whatever reason.
He was slaughtered,
hung, drawn and quartered,
In a barbarous inhuman way
He was beheaded this one August day.

This landowners son still lives on
The spirit of him hasn't gone,
In every Scot who is born

And then draws their first breath
William Wallace lives on after death.

One ruin always makes me think that it was of some
importance. Research has found that it is Collairnie Castle.
Apparently it was a tower house with a courtyard
surrounded by walls; built in the 15th century and Mary
Queen of Scots stayed there for three nights on her journey
to St Andrews. One Sunday afternoon in my sunny Codsall
conservatory whilst reading up on the castle I found that
amongst the coat of arms that was once displayed in the
lower room is Trail of Blebo. I have Trail and Traill in my
line; there is someone more knowledgable than me that will
find good reason to know that we are in that coat of arms;
once displayed in Collairnie Castle. (Apologies for the poor
artwork as I am out of practice and don't want to breach
copyright laws). Trail motto – Discrimine Salus; which
means judge carefully.

It was a grey mid-afternoon in north east Fife as we drove
back from Perth on the B937 alongside Lindores Loch.
Nearing the end at the junction of the A91 is a left turn that
takes you into a hamlet that in my lifetime will be forever in
my heart. It seems a long time ago since we first visited here
when its air of peacefulness was met with disbelief. That is
because I couldn't believe that we have a connection to
here.

For about 15 minutes we were parked on the grass verge
outside of the farm in Collessie where my dad was born. To

visit here is a ritual of mine and there has been four cars that have taken part in this journey. Suddenly out of the drive came two lassies on a quad bike pulling a trailer carrying a couple of ewes and their spring lambs. The farmer or a worker had parked up an agricultural machine near the road and was in the opposite field hammering at something. Within minutes the lassies returned minus the load and turned into the gate at Halhill Farm. Little did they know how much a farm outreach worker there in the 1920's played on my mind. Lynne told me that the farmer kept giving me an inquisitive look and was expecting me to engage in conversation. I would gladly have done so but was engrossed in writing this paragraph whilst resting on a Collessie wall. Visibility was poor on this March day in late 2017 and the Lomonds had a look of being faded artistically into a painting. I could make out Collessie church and then noticed that I had another inquisitive onlooker. There in the field was a lone sheep; half turned and I could read its thought of "what's he up to?"

Collessie

'I rested a while
by the kirk yard wall
square tower and spire,
standing tall'

My mind went back to that Spring day in 2002 when first visiting Collessie. My wife Lynne, elder brother Gareth and myself strolled about this hamlet that has a conservation status (areas of special architectural or historic interest, the character or appearance of which it is desirable to preserve or enhance). I would be in my late forties and it was in disbelief that I realised we had a connection to here. My thoughts just tumbled along in the Den Burn that we were looking on that runs through Collessie.

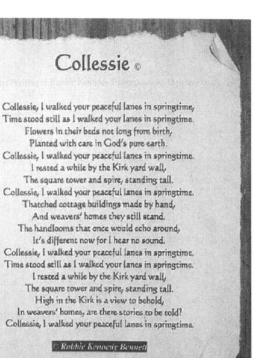

Collessie ©

Collessie, I walked your peaceful lanes in springtime,
Time stood still as I walked your lanes in springtime.
Flowers in their beds not long from birth,
Planted with care in God's pure earth.
Collessie, I walked your peaceful lanes in springtime.
I rested a while by the Kirk yard wall,
The square tower and spire, standing tall.
Collessie, I walked your peaceful lanes in springtime.
Thatched cottage buildings made by hand,
And weavers' homes they still stand.
The handlooms that once would echo around,
It's different now for I hear no sound.
Collessie, I walked your peaceful lanes in springtime.
Time stood still as I walked your lanes in springtime.
I rested a while by the Kirk yard wall,
The square tower and spire, standing tall.
High in the Kirk is a view to behold,
In weavers' homes, are there stories to be told?
Collessie, I walked your peaceful lanes in springtime.

© Robbie Kennedy Bennett

Looking at a map I see that it starts on higher ground east of Woodmill Farm as Black Burn; weaving its way through Collessie, crossing the A91 and through the dividing land at Birnie Loch. It runs out of there by Kinloch as Collessie Burn as if it has the right to claim the name. Near to Easter Kilwhiss Farm it changes to Rossie Drain; finally giving into the River Eden west of Lathrisk. It can be said that the burn runs much further than that; because I study that map and write these words one early Sarurday morning on my ipad in a darkened bedroom of my Staffordshire home.

Alex later sent me a photo of the house that his great uncle stayed in with his great granny Rodgers standing outside. He also told me "My mum, dad and I used to stay on the top storey, accessed from up the brae a little and along the lane in front of the church wall; the house is all one now."

We stopped by at Monimail as we were driving that way as I remembered that Alex Kennedy had told me that his Scott grandparents were at rest there. It was very quiet and peaceful in what I have found these Fife villages to be. It is a small cemetery and Lawrence T. Scott and his wife Helen W. Rodgers were discovered. Next to them was John Rodgers, Lomond View, Collessie. This would be the great uncle that Alex told me of when first visiting our house earlier in the month. There was also some Traill headstones and I can recall Jane, Alex's mom, saying in one of his emails that 'she knew a Traill laddie who worked on the coal lorry that visited Collessie.' One would like to find if there is a link to our line.

Just as Lynne and I were getting into the car I noticed Monimail Old Parish Church opposite. Little remains of the building which went out of use in 1796 and me being not one to drive away without a wee browse; I was soon over the road to what looked like a burial ground and I didn't even get through the gate without spotting a name.

Whenever searching on the Internet for Bennet, Ladybank; names appear with one 't' at the end and sometimes two. Ours was one when we were in Dundee and came down to Fife. In fact a branch that went to Toronto in Canada still has only one. There's a fallen soldier that keeps on showing in my search and appears with both (t&tt) as does his father: this is most frustrating when trying to find if there is a link. Well my question was answered because on that gate pillar is a war plaque with the name Pte. Adam Addison Bennett. He died in 1915; the son of William & Annie Munro Bennett of Melville Gardens, Ladybank, Fife. Not a known relation but you still have my deepest respect sir.

Since writing the paragraph above I found a post on a forum from 2007. This lady is a grandaughter of the brother of Adam. It was whilst doing her family tree that his death was discovered. She was saddened to think that he died aged 23 and not remembered in the family. It's not my place to say if that was true or not; but is that what the Great War did to families? Was there so many soldiers giving their life and the news an everyday occurrence: did families have to suffer in almost silence? The post was 10 years old but I still looked to no avail to see if an email address had been displayed. If so I would have messaged her to say that Pte. Adam Addison Bennett, your grandads brother has been remembered here and now.

My Tale of Writing Elizabeth Wallace Traill

'there's your name in the sand;
my writing with
a piece of driftwood in my hand'

When returning to my ancestral St Andrews; every day brings the same but yet different thoughts. Places, people, circumstances of a time that plays heavily on my mind. I walk, stop and write something of what or whoever comes to mind. I was down on the East Sands and thought of Elizabeth, sister of my great grandmother. I made my way through the harbour as sparrows were busy in the lobster cages. Suddenly I was a few feet away from the heron that I often see, he was side on but I could tell that I was well in sight. I got closer, too close so he set flight. Up by the castle ruins I got writing again; this time sparrows were again leading vocally. An hour later I was back on the sand, this time my writing of her name was blessed with sunshine.

My Tale of Writing
Elizabeth Wallace Traill ©

2017

Elizabeth Wallace Traill
I have little facts to write,
caught in a reverie not long from first light
here in St Andrews.

Seaweed leaves a trace
of where the tide has been,
there beyond a grassy bank

are o'er a hundred years between
aye, 'tween you and I, time went by.

Elizabeth Wallace Traill
there's your name in the sand;
my writing with a piece of driftwood in my hand
there in all its glory by the sea.

Elizabeth Wallace Traill
I go to destroy my scribe but leave it be,
for any beachcomber if they choose
to read Elizabeth Wallace Traill
of Dundee and St Andrews.

Elizabeth Wallace Traill
too young really
someone loved you dearly,
without doubt, when prematurely
your flame went out.

I wander awa' and find myself at the castle railing wall
looking down North Caste Street;
in thought Elizabeth, you and I we meet;
interrupted we were as sparrows playfully tweet
loudly; in greenery growing within twenty five feet;
entertaining they be; Elizabeth come and see.

Elizabeth Wallace Traill
to visit your stone, I never fail,
when time to depart
I leave with a heavy ancestral heart.

Elizabeth Wallace Traill
I jump down from that grassy bank and land,
sun now shines on your name in the sand;
my writing from a piece of driftwood in my hand
there by the sea.

Elizabeth Wallace Traill
a dearly beloved daughter
aged only twenty four,
when you passed through heavens door.

Seaweed leaves a trace
how I wish to see your young sweet face,
as for your name by the shore
tonight the tide shall take o'er.

Handling the Very Same Stone

'there's no wonder that St Andrews feels like home'

The East Sands, St Andrews and I am within a short distance of my great grandmothers birthplace. In the photographic black and white world of the old days that you see in pictures, it is easy for me to imagine her and her brothers and sisters on this beach. They would've heard the same sound of waves and gulls and felt the sea breeze in their faces. I make that vision seem as if it's a reality and can now add true modern memories. Our son Steven and Aaron his eldest child stepping on that sand for the first time. Caitlyn still a toddler being pushed along the path in her pram. Four years later we had Liam and Kiera-Marie playing on the sand and braving the ice cold sea. This being a beach that I was not to know that we had so much of a close connection to. On the sand are the usual stones that wash in and out with the tide; now there's a thought?

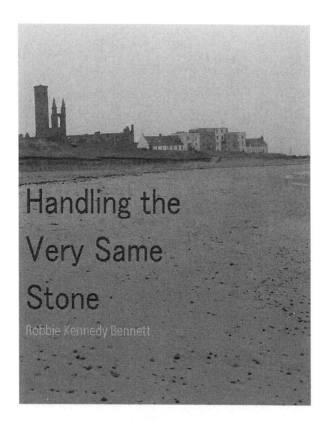

Handling the
Very Same
Stone

Robbie Kennedy Bennett

Handling the Very Same Stone ©

2017

Isabella and your siblings
did you ever play?
on the sand where I stand
that's hard to walk away.

There a fishermans daughter
goes running to the water,
and a fishermans son
were you on there having fun?

On the same sand
what's the chance of us
handling the very same stone,
there's no wonder that
St Andrews feels like home.

I hear bairns laughter
lassies and laddies loving the sea,
aye there's no wonder that
St Andrews feels like home to me.

Isabella and your siblings
now I must leave,
the late eighteen hundreds are
tucked safely in my sleeve.

Suddenly the beach is empty
the sand is bare,
Isabella and your siblings
were you really there?

All is quiet, distant and calm
unexplainable that there in my palm,
and what's the chance of us
handling the very same stone,
there's no wonder that
St Andrews feels like home.

Kilted by the Tay

'Black Watch soldier
you stand before
armed for combat
prepared to draw'

The Tay is forever in the history of not only the picturesque
views, being the longest river on the British Isles and the
living that it gave to many a scottish family. I must add
mine to that huge amount of clan and kin that owes a lot to.
On Wednesday 29th March 2017 my cousin Paul and his
partner Jacqui had invited us out to accompany them to
Aberfeldy, what is a burgh in Perth and Kinross. This is a
small highland town where they lived 17 years before and
Jacqui is mentioned on a board at the golf club by General
Wade's bridge alongside the Tay in gold lettering as club
captain in 1999 and Paul was the golf professional. There
are pictures on the club wall of when there was floods and
the devastation that it caused. Across the road is also an

impressive Black Watch monument, a regiment that is always coming to the forefront of the Scottish family members of mine.

'Black Watch soldier
kilted by the Tay
peace in the Highlands
watch upon the brae'

Kilted
by
the
Tay.©

Robbie Kennedy Bennett

Kilted by the Tay ©

2017

Black Watch soldier
you stand before
armed for combat
prepared to draw.

Black Watch soldier
an undress cap you wear
feathered proudly
high o'er you stare

Black Watch soldier
kilted by the Tay
peace in the Highlands
watch upon the brae.

Surprisingly as I entered the club that a pint of beer was waiting for me. I was taking photos of the statue and thought that they were searching for somewhere for a cup of tea.

Returning to the Tay, earlier we had spent time at Taymouth Castle estate and an hour at the Kenmore, the eastern point of Loch Tay. We had our homemade lunches alongside the loch and we appeared to be popular guests as we became very good friends of a flock of ducks which could also be named something else depending on what research mode you consider it to be. It was here in Kenmore that Paul wanted to show me the Robbie Burns poem from 1787 pencilled on the wall. It was amusing as four of us walked inside, disturbed a dog whose water bowl was beneath the poem on the wall and walked out again without having a drink.

The road back to Fife was drizzly and we walked the streets of Dunkeld eating gorgeous haddock and chips from a tray. I caught sight of a road sign to Luncarty and recalled the time that Lynne and I we were drawn to.There is a view that I found that this is where our Bennet's married with Stewart are from; the other being Angus; both hold good reason to believe that they are correct.

We travelled south and caught up with the Tay at Perth and if correct that in that belief flowed with us sailing for Dundee.

The Very Moment of the Reading of Their Name

*'the years of sadness,
the families pain,
clouds over me then falls
like pouring rain'*

Our next day Lynne and I were in Dundee which turned out to be better weather wise. I love the approach from Fife as the Law appears like a the leading star at a show. What's satisfying now is that I know I made the effort last year and was at the summit on a fine, clear morning. The view was amazing as the sun appeared out in the east and lightened up another ancestral home of mine.

During a break in shopping we made our way to St Andrew's Parish Church in close vicinity to where my

228

ancestors lived. I look up the church pathway and wonder if any of them were ever inside for a service. Recently I posted a poem and picture of the church on social media and an important fact came about. In September 1970 the church spire was struck by lightning. Masonry fell through the roof and for safety purpose part of the spire was dismantled. Pictures of that time show how damaged it was and of course I appeared all 'clever like' when explaining the story to Lynne.

I noticed that the church door was open and took this as an opportunity to go and take a look inside. Just then a countless stream of school children and teachers exited the church which was apparently their end of term Easter service. After what seemed like ages and a wonder how they all fitted in; I was kindly allowed to enter for a few minutes. The stained glass windows were colourful and bright and I turned down the offer of going on the balcony to take a picture. I could see that they were clearing up after the service and did not want to be in their way. I couldn't leave though without reading the names of those who fell for our freedom. I did notice that there are two Anderson's but it is not known if they are related. On a board alongside the red rampant lion on a St Andrews flag; 'TO THE PRAISE OF GOD AND IN GRATEFUL MEMORY OF THE MEN OF THIS CONGREGATION WHO GAVE THEIR LIVES IN THE GREAT

WAR 1914-18 THE ORGAN OF THIS CHURCH IS
DEDICATED. There then follows two lines of fallen solders
and beneath them; "HE HATH PUT A NEW SONG IN MY
MOUTH"

The
Very
Moment
of the
Reading
of Their
Name

The Very Moment of
the Reading of Their Name ©

2017

All cities, towns, villages, I stop and pause,
where there's names, fallen heroes of the cause;
the years of sadness, the families pain,
clouds over me then falls like pouring rain.
In some strange way they somehow rise again
in the very moment of the reading of their name,
every letter should be scrutinised and read
even though joined together they are dead,
but that very moment of the reading of their name,
rise again, fallen heroes, rise again.

Kennedy, Trail, Bennet

'names play games
their blood does
runs through my veins'

I have a copy of a letter sent to my mom answering questions of dads start in life. It's been in the family for years and occasionally I read it in search of certain details that I need reassuring or may have missed. This letter is on my ipad and one Thursday morning I am lying in bed of our caravan. I zoomed into a line to see how Bennet had been written. The family name of Trail was before it, only one 't' at the end for some reason. In the line above the last letter of our name of Kennedy joins into the line below. I have never noticed that before and studying closely it looks like Bennet is jumping through a loop with Trail about to follow. I have researched plenty of times into all of these three names and still they play games.

Kennedy, Trail, Bennet ©

2017

Names play games
their blood does
runs through my veins
but still they play games

They hide
then they startle me
from deep inside

They scatter
and run away,
knowing I'll be searching
'till the end of my day.

Duff and Anderson of Kingsbarns

'Kingsbarns, oh Kingsbarns, how your church bells did surprise'

The church clock in Kingsbarns struck for midday which for a moment caught me by surprise. I was totally concentrating on looking for names and tried to hide my embarrassment just in case anyone noticed me. The bend in the road of Kingsbarns adds to the character and the inn next door is inviting but as of yet it has not had yours truly as a customer. Showers of rain were coming and going but not like the last time we were here as it was quite a torrential downpour forcing Lynne and myself to abort our search and hurry back to the car. Thinking back about those church bells make me wonder if they rang out for the wedding of Peter Anderson and Ann Brown Duff who married in this parish in 1880 or was it on the farm of Randerton that they were wed? Their daughter Agnes was born here and in ancestral terms would be my great grandmother. Unfortunately I found that she died in her early thirties.

Duff and Anderson
of Kingsbarns ©

Robbie Kennedy Bennett

Duff and Anderson of Kingsbarns ©

2017

In the parish of Kingsbarns

there the banns were heard,

listening hard enough

for every proclamation word

for Ann Duff and Peter Anderson

all was silent where they sing, they pray,

then bells chimed for mid-day

causing an awaking alarm

arm in arm at Randerton Farm

listening hard enough

for every proclamation word

for Ann Duff and Peter Anderson

Kingsbarns, oh Kingsbarns,

how your church bells did surprise;

this laddie auld and wise

a laddie he tells no lies

in his auld imaginary room

he sees a bride and her groom

in the parish of Kingsbarns

they're here, we're here

to hear the reading of the banns

for Ann Duff and Peter Anderson

of Kingsbarns, oh Kingsbarns

Giffordtown,
ay Ye I've Heard

'here listening tae th' soond ay a bird singing sweetly, aye sae sweetly'

Not long after we were further inland at the junction of Angle Park which is a track that leads to Birns Farm near Giffordtown. A few minutes earlier the war memorial at the hall of that name drew my attention and soon I was out there taking photos of names of the fallen. I seemed to recall dad mentioning Giffordtown.

Once more the auld thinking head clicks into gear suggesting that it would be a good idea if I found out more about Giffordtown. In 2004 they commemorated the 150th anniversary of the now named Giffordtown Village Hall. Originally it was a Free Church School saving children the walking journey to Collessie or Ladybank. The building fell into disuse until 1919 when a group of local dignitaries purchased it from the United Free Church.

My Bennet's were living in Ladybank at that time and I am certain that they would be aware of this. I can't help but wonder if a young Kennedy lassie attended here?

The hall then became a recreation club disbanding at the time of the Second World War. For the next 30 years the hall did not obtain its former worth until 1973. Reverend Alexander Philp the minister of Ladybank had an influential involvement in what is now Giffordtown Village Hall.

I have learned plenty about Fife this past decade and a half but I feel as though I am only scratching the surface. It was a strange ancestral, rural feeling just to be in that place and taking a photograph with the name of Giffordtown in the picture.

We couldn't see a sign of the farm except that of a boarding kennels and cattery. Jane, mother of Alex Kennedy who we recently met believes that Peter Anderson and his wife Ann stayed at this farm. I ventured just a short way down the track and the view of a small loch with the Lomond Hills in the background was fantastic. Once again I felt fortunate to have a connection to the Kingdom of Fife.

Giffordtown, ay Ye I've Heard ©

2017

Giffordtown, ay ye I've heard
here listening tae th' soond ay a bird
singing sweetly, aye sae sweetly,
here in Giffordtown.
Giffordtown, I know your name
don't know why, nae not why,
as th' bird tha' sings sae sweetly
awa' it does fly, from Giffordtown.
Giffordtown, I hear your song,
nae, not wrong, shall not dwell,
but let me tell, I see your sign,
an' hear a voice ay mine, saying Giffordtown.
Then children, distant children,
singing sweetly, aye sae sweetly in Giffordtown.

I Gave My All
For Cupar Hearts

'giving me time o' plenty
I dreamt last night
that I was around mid twenty'

What often confuses me is when I see the 'Bow of Fife' and 'Howe of Fife;' where exactly are they and what do they mean?

I presume that the Howe of Fife is the low lying hollow agricultural land north of the Lomonds. I have always thought it to be the central area but apparently my research finds that it could be classed further east, west and north. The Bow of Fife has also got me wanting to find the actual place or where it starts and finishes?

Once again I found it to be clear as mud because it could be the bending of the road or from an old farmers phrase when pricing grain (bolls sounding like bows). It is also

243

thought that a few dwellings, 'the Bow of Fife,' on the road
to Cupar is the exact centre of Fife.

So to get on with this writing' I drove through the Bow of
Fife in the Howe of Fife straight into a dream of mine in
Cupar; the one time busy market town with its former royal
burgh and parish. I was into the shopping area near St
John's on Bonnygate and noticed that there was a name
change (not yet joined with Dairsie pre 2005). Opposite
was the watchmaker and jeweller Thomas Young, (a
surname from Bilston in Lynne's family). That shop front
looked the same (family business on Bonnygate since 1956,
Thomas Young started as an apprentice in 1947 at
Ladybank in his uncle Robert Kemlo's workshop – would be
interesting to find where that was?).

The traffic was still and I glanced up at the sloping shop
roof. A two story building sandwiched in between three
story either side. It had a look of a wee person fighting and
winning to keep its space.

I stopped at a crossing to allow pedestrians to change sides.
There wasn't a traffic light, just an amber flashing ball on a
black and white pole. People looked and dressed different, a
mother pushing a baby in an old fashioned pram. I checked
my mirror to see behind me and caught sight of myself as a

younger man. I went to pull away, then a couple of blokes as if in a hurry ran in front of me over the crossing; followed by an elderly and out of breath third: one of them wearing a brown pin-stripe suit carrying an Adidas bag, he was that younger man I saw in my drivers mirror.

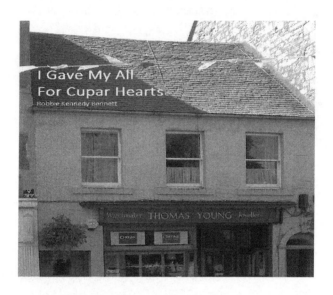

I Gave My All For Cupar Hearts ©

2017

I dreamt last night that I was around mid twenty
on a train near to the entry of
Edinburgh Waverley Station
there was I with a beating chest
as Cupar Hearts had made a request
for me to play as a guest
in one heck of an important game
they had noticed my name from around these parts
I received a letter from Cupar Hearts
not giving me time o' plenty

I dreamt last night that I was around mid twenty

Changing trains at Edinburgh to get to Cupar in about one
hour
I was twenty something or other
there a travelling without another
giving me time o' plenty
I dreamt last night that I was around mid twenty

In my bag was pads and boots
at Ladybank there my strong roots
that train it seemed to stop a long, long time
then off it went to Cupar further on down the line

I dreamt last night that I was around mid twenty
on a train near to the entry of Cupar Railway Station
where a relation was awaiting my kind of homecoming
then I saw someone running and waving plenty
I dreamt last night that I was around mid twenty

My boots and pads were in my bag
not was it heavy or did drag
out of Cupar Railway Station
there I walked with my relation

Words were spoke but nothing heard said

all that was racing in my head
is that I hope I play my very best
as Cupar Hearts had made that request
for me to play as a guest
in one heck of an important game

Pointed out was Railway Place
my beating heart it seemed to race
perhaps just strong and proud
as I felt it drumming plenty
I dreamt last night that I was around mid twenty

We crossed South Bridge and up Crossgate
not time to stop as we were late
we'd got to be at the mercat cross
it was there I met presumably the boss
for authority was in the air
we hurried on with little time to spare

He gave me a shirt of claret and blue
I thought of Villains and Hammers too
he barked "all you who starts,
give you're all for the Cupar Hearts"

Ninety minutes soon went by
I scored a goal beneath a Fife sky

and life was feeling great
"c'mon" came a shout "you're going to be late"

I left behind that brilliant match
down Crossgate for my train to catch
I glanced again at Railway Place
and wished to see a face
and a loving smile, so that I could leave Cupar in style
not giving me time o' plenty
I dreamt last night that I was around mid twenty

To my relation there was a fond farewell
and then at Ladybank, there was as well
this time we didn't seem to stop as long
still, feelings were painful, they were strong
I was twenty something or other
there a travelling without another
Soon the Forth Bridge came in view
then Edinburgh and Waverley too,
asleep I fell on a homebound train
dreaming plenty....
I dreamt last night that I was around mid twenty

I woke this morning aged sixty plus two
that dream felt real that I had been through
downstairs in the kitchen a boiling kettle starts

I gave my all for Cupar Hearts
"if only this was all true, aye, sleepy old you"

I shall dream tonight or at least try again
to recapture being mid twenty
and on that Edinburgh train....

Ordinary Items Such as Sand and Staine

'was kind Rab oh sae kind
for ye tae spend yer time an' find'

I go for months on end without seeing the coast and I miss it greatly. Not the razzle dazzle and bright lights but the naturalness of it all. There's something inside of me when in Fife that tells that all before me has been seen in previous years by kin of mine. Once I find where my ancestors came from it makes an impression on me. I was a middle aged man before I found all these coastal links that I have. It's no wonder as a lad that I loved the seaside holidays mostly in Gt Yarmouth. When we arrived I couldn't get to the beach fast enough. Walking the Fife Coastal Path in 2007–08 will stay with me forever when the coastline views as far as the eye could see were sensational. Another feeling is that my ancestors would be pleased that a descendant of theirs came back to where they spent or ended their days. It's never more stronger that being on the East Sands at St Andrews with the Eastern Cemetery in view.

The first day of the month and my last morning walk was coming to an end. My thoughts were on family back home in Wolverhampton and looking forward to seeing the grandchildren. As I walked out of the Pends into Shorehead, Isabella Cramond Traill's birthplace, the name of 'Boy Aaron' on a boat caught my attention. The holiday week of ours started on his 10th birthday so it seemed fitting to look ahead to our departure from St Andrews. The wash of the waves was on the East Sands made a soothing, tranquil sound; that shall have to be all, until the next time

Ordinary Items Such as Sand and Staine

Robbie Kennedy Bennett

Ordinary Items Such as
Sand and Staine ©

2017

Ye wilnae forget us Rab will ye?
nae let us fade an' be out o' yer mind,
was kind Rab oh sae kind
for ye tae spend yer time an' find.
Aye tae find Rab where we had our days
yer just like us in sae many ways,
been a pleasure Rab a real pleasure
an' there's nae pot o' gold, nae treasure,
for ye tae fill yer pockets an' sack;
Rab, are ye' gonna cam back?
tae th' ordinary items such as sand and staine
Rab, are ye gonna cam hame?

Come Here
Fallen Soldier

"nae lad that's far fetched"
but the branches
look like arms out stretched'

I would love to turn the clock back to 1930 and go walking about the pine trees at Monkstown Wood. Dad would be a laddie and about to start his adventures here. Older Bennet's in the family would have a story or two to tell. There's a call, we turn around and see a young man about aged 20. It was Thomas Loch Traill Bennet and he was coming to see if we were alright. He led us to old hiding places of his and told us what to look and listen for. I feel as if I know him now instead of discovering his name on a headstone in Kingskettle dated 1933. He was named after a soldier in our family who I found on the war memorial in St Andrews.

Each time we are nearing the finale to our trip to Fife we stop by at Ladybank. It's easy for me to imagine my Bennet's walking about here. The finding and pride that I have knowing that we have a connection through Hector Bennet in helping to raise funds for this war memorial. He would I presume have seen the unveiling of this remembrance and stood in silence many times.

Lynne and I called into Ladybank twice this week and both times purchased something from the butchers. We went over the road and sat on a bench in the Haig Memorial Garden.

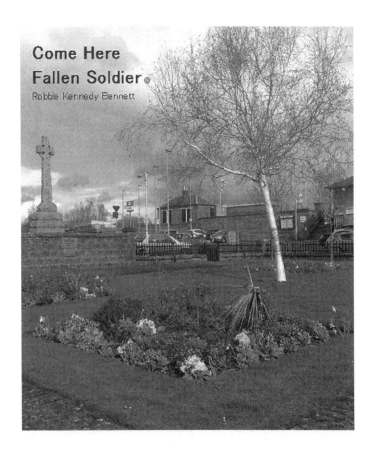

Come Here
Fallen Soldier©

Robbie Kennedy Bennett

Come Here Fallen Soldier ©

2017

In the Haig Memorial Garden, Ladybank
a silver birch does lean,
appearing a wee bit to be reaching
may be to me it is teaching.

"Nae lad that's far fetched"
but the branches look like arms out stretched,
arms outstretched to collect those men who fell
for a man like me to read and tell.

"Nae lad that's nae right"
but to ask is quite polite
to keep in sight and at arms length
the bravery and inner strength
to overcome their fear.

As a silver birch near says
"come here fallen soldier, come here."

A Kirkcaldy Man Named Kennedy

'our freedom came at a cost
many a life was horribly lost'

There is evidence of fallen soldiers who protected these shores all around the United Kingdom. We choose to read the names on the memorials or not but I certainly do especially when in Fife. My writing and ancestral interest has unearthed names in my bloodline that I didn't know of. Thomas Loch Traill in St Andrews, brother of my gt grandmother Isabella. Dr Ian Traill went further than my discovery and found him to be at rest in the USA after his immigration there. Another fascinating and sad finding came one festive period when another name entered into a search engine on the Internet answered plenty of my questions. I was drawn to Fife even more by these gallant men that I am related to. It was fascinating enough to find him on a plaque in Abbotshall Parish Church a few years ago; now there was another story simmering on the ancestral stove.

ROBERT CUNNINGHAM
YORKSHIRE REGT.
DAVID SHIELDS, SGT.
LANCASHIRE FUS.
ALEXANDER KENNEDY, PTE.
ALEXANDER WEEPERS, PTE.
ROYAL SCOTS FUS.
WILLIAM BLACKWOOD, L/CPL.
JOHN CAIRD, PTE.
HARRY CHALMERS, SGT.
DAVID GORMIE, PTE.

A Kirkcaldy Man Named Kennedy ©
Remembrance Day 2015

There at rest is a man named Kennedy
I found that he lies in the ground in France,
if I have the chance one day my Kennedy
I shall pay respect to you in France.

Until then brave sir may I say
there shall be thoughts of you and your Salford Pals
on Remembrance Day

Our freedom came at a cost
many a life was horribly lost,
a long thoughtful minute of silence it shall be
for a Kirkcaldy man named Kennedy.

SOLDIER, KIRKCALDY SOLDIER

'ne'er did you come home
or grow older
Soldier,
Kirkcaldy Soldier'

Saturday morning 1st April 2017 marked the 100 year anniversary of when the 16th Lancashire Fusiliers (2nd Salford Pals) were in action at Savy Wood.

My writing has unearthed many findings that I would not have known otherwise. One being to Foreste Communal Cemetery in France.

The paragraph below is from the CWGC;

'Foreste is a village in the Department of the Aisne, situated approximately 14 kilometres west of St. Quentin and approximately 9 kilometres north of Ham. Foreste

Communal Cemetery is situated to the south of the village on the D34. Foreste Communal Cemetery was used by the 92nd Field Ambulance in April 1917 and later by the 61st (South Midland) Division. The village fell into German hands in the summer of 1918. The cemetery contains 117 Commonwealth burials and commemorations of the First World War. 22 of the burials are unidentified and special memorials are erected to 23 casualties buried by the Germans whose grave cannot be traced.'

Private Alexander Kennedy, son of Mr. and Mrs. Alexander Kennedy, of Kirkcaldy; husband of the late Agnes Duff Anderson Kennedy, of Kirkcaldy, Fife, is one of those soldiers and from who I descend.

It is worth mentioning at this point that at the time of writing the poem there had not been any previous conversation or meeting with anyone of my Kennedy side.

As told in earlier pages my poem 'Soldier, Kirkcaldy Soldier' was seen and a comment made on a Fife Facebook page for Remembrance Sunday 2016 by another Alex Kennedy. Remarkably it was found that we are related through that Lancashire Fusilier, both being great grandsons, and have met each other twice since then. We shall do so again today and together visit the war memorial in Kirkcaldy before my journey back to Codsall.

My wife Lynne and I was pleasantly surprised when
arriving at Alex and Margaret's home in Kirkcaldy to find
that their son Grant was joining us in the 100 year tribute.
Grant being a great, great grandson of this soldier.

We were positioning ourselves for photographs as church
bells were sounding for midday which added to the
occasion. I was aware that the battalion assembled at
1.00pm and on that fatal day in 1917 it was lashing down
with rain, sleet and snow. One hundred years on it was a
fine bright day in Private Alexander Kennedy's hometown
of Kirkcaldy. 'SOLDIER, KIRKCALDY SOLDIER' is a poem
that I am extremely proud of, that made this event happen.

Shortly afterwards the story above and the following
picture made the Black Country Bugle.

Pictured from left to right, Alex Kennedy, Grant Kennedy and myself Robbie Kennedy Bennett.

Avise la Fin

Th' Callin' o' Fife

'Finally, aye

finally,

th' ancestral

callin' o' Fife '

A Thursday morning in April 2017 and I had just been driving through my old area on the east of Wolverhampton towards Tipton and deeper into what they call the Black Country. It was good to see my marathon training roads of the past and not forgetting the courting journey I made when meeting Lynne at her home in Parkfields. When nearing Coseley Working Mens club I thought of the photo of my dad with his thumb up when he was driving a Delta lorry for the carnival. I passed over the brow of the hill on the Birmingham New Road and Dudley Castle came into view. Suddenly observing the vehicle in front of me I noticed that it displayed the Saltire flag of Scotland. How strange as this is exactly as to why I was heading for Tipton.

brought
together,
me and
mine
locked
together in
a Scottish
Wulfrunian
time.

I parked up at the cemetery and settled for a few minutes to write the above which believe it or not is a link to St Andrews in Fife. Something caught my eye and as I looked out of the car window, a heron was walking amongst grave stones. Remember the heron from St Andrews Harbour; I wondered if it had followed me from there to Tipton?

It was a stroke of luck that I found the gravestone of John Percy Clark so quickly. My distant relative and fellow Traill descendant Ian Traill is working on a book of that family. He had sent me a link to a picture of JPC's final resting place and names are close to the one in our line who married a Traill.

Tipton cemetery is enormous and it would be very difficult to find. Upon studying the photo I could make out that the stone was near to a curb and a car park. Further more in the background was the name of a shop which I googled and found the postcode of. Within minutes of my arrival the grave in question was found; all because of my amateur detective skills. Whether or not this John Percy Clark is ours; in which a few weeks later it turned out not to be; it was still an interesting find to bring St Andrews in Fife to Tipton in the West Midlands.

James Traill and Elizabeth Brown, this gt grandson of your daughter Isabella had you in mind once more. For a moment I could see the East Sands from their stone in St Andrews.

Isabella I Hear You Cry ©

2017

In the year of zero one you lost a sister dear
that's what I'm realising sadly standing here;
then when nineteen came a brother of your name.
Twenty four your father, twenty five your mother too;
Oh Isabella, Isabella I feel sad for you.
The sea I hear washes away that tear,
I place my hand, as always, when I say goodbye;
but oh Isabella, Isabella I hear you cry.

For some reason I keep on going back to Fife; drawn by the past and building a future. There's a familiarity now about certain villages and towns plus the memories made of the last decade and half. I could stay here for longer spells than a holiday of a week at a time. Perhaps rent a cottage for a month in the East Neuk; "aye that would be grand" said the Fifer in me. Just think Rab, waking up and opening the curtains to see the North Sea. Put on my boots and go walking for hours. The simple, taking for granted enjoyment of sight. Returning to that wee cottage for breakfast; again with sea in view. We'd stroll Lynne and I just as we did about Parkfields when we were teenagers. Evening time as the sun is setting in the west; there'd be sparkling on the water; listening to the waves gently taking their turn to roll over and wash sand and stones; the simple, taking for granted enjoyment of hearing.

I study names in my family tree and randomly go surfing the internet. Some are found and others not. I see place names where they were born or married; that in itself creates a story in me. I may know where mentioned or I may not; when found, my ancestral engine clicks into gear.

"Surely we're connected to the Earl of Fife," says that Fifer inside once more. He's always coming up with these type of thoughts and gets me looking. It is true that we have the name Duff starting with dads birth mother going back I found at least seven generations. First names of John and James Duff carried down the line from at least the late 1600's to about 1862 when females Ann, Agnes and Annie took over. Again that Fifer spouts up "if we're not directly connected to the Earl of Fife, we must be close cousins!"

I made a phone call on Easter Sunday, nothing unusual in that you may think but it was where I made that call to. Dad was born on Halhill Farm, Collessie and I needed to enquire who the current owner is. A lady answered and put me on to Willie Barr who confirmed it was him. I explained as best that I could; that I was writing a book and wanted to put a photo of myself taken outside his farm on the front cover. He granted the permission but asked me if I could send him the photo on an email.

Mr Barr also showed interest in this request and asked me what year this would have been. When I told him it was 1926 he immediately knew that Halhill at that time was owned by the Storer's who are now at Rossie Farm in Auchtermuchty. I was tempted to carry on our telephone conversation but declined to do so as I was aware that I had called uninvited. I appreciated being told by Mr Barr that his grandfather took on Halhill Farm in 1943.

There's a guilty feeling inside of me that I didn't get to know my roots in Fife earlier than I did. Was I ignorant to the fact perhaps; or not encouraged or forced to learn?

A realisation that surfaced somewhere near middle aged and took over. To let a person live and die without knowing who they are isn't right and doesn't fit nicely; especially if it is a parent; I was fortunate with mom but with dad, I feel as if I did not show enough interest.

There's more feelings than sound, brought on by sight; there's a hurt that won't go away. I was 'pipped at the post,' 'if you snooze you lose;' 'I missed a sitter!' There you go, I was too wrapped up in sport!

Hardly anything to listen to, just the joy of seeing agricultural beauty in the Howe of Fife. It's March, it was September the last time, reminds me that we must plan for the next time.

I can just about see the Lomonds, not as clear as the last time; I wonder how clear they were when a bairn in arms came out of the gate near to where I stand. Whoever glanced at the Lomonds would be looking over my head. It's the last week in March, same as it was when; way back then; aye, the same but somewhat different.

'To hear your song is wonderful, but when the song is undressed without the word; the tune softens, that's when your song is heard.'

At the time of writing there has been three representatives of our Scottish bloodline that have visited my home. Dr Ian Traill in 2016 who is a grandson of John Grace Wallace Traill, brother of my great grandmother Isabella Cramond Traill and in 2017 Alex Kennedy who is a grandson of Alexander Kennedy, brother of my dads birthmother Annie Duff Kennedy. He died in 1977 aged 77 and Alex would later send me a picture of his headstone in Markinch. I wonder if he ever saw my dad, his nephew as a new bairn?

In June 2017 Dr Ian Traill once again with Jean Bronstein his elder sister. They were at the end of their ancestral holiday in Scotland having left Dundee with their parents in 1954. Ian lives in Changsha, China and Jean in Melbourne, Australia.

Before their departure photographs were taken of us all

outside with photographic views of the Auld Grey Toon.

If only there in my St Andrews Square of my Staffordshire back garden could we be joined by some of them old Dundonians and Fifers. Aye they'd smile and tell me that I had done well to find them. "We tried uir best tae hide laddie," they underestimate the enthusiasm that I have for certain tasks. The mental strength that pushes me on. "Pish laddie!" (meaning nonsense) "ye nae fin' us aw!" How right they were as they laughed and toasted those who are still in hiding. I laughed with them!

We looked at the picture that I have blown up on the north fence. They can see that it is the East Sands and the harbour. One mentions that the middle buildings have been replaced but not both ends where the pubs were. They look east and see the sunrise on the North Sea on my Staffordshire fence. All of them I noticed had hard working hands, both man and woman. Caledonia is sung on the radio, they hadn't heard it before as it was after their time. They ask me to tell them about Isaiah Owen, and his family from Wolverhampton; so I do so and that he has a gt grandson named Paul who is a caddie at St Andrews. "Ah kent Auld Tam Morris" I heard shout.

One of them came out the house with a picture in hand. "Is

thes uir kin?" "Aye" said another, "that's uir Cecil." Then I
was asked to read out the poem in the frame, again I do so;
afterwards a song about Jimmy Shand the accordion man
played out on the radio. Some of the above is true and some
wishful thinking!

THE KINGDOM OF FIFE ©

2002

It's pleasing to be where you've been,
And to see what you've seen,
The fields of farmers corn,
The cottage in where you were born,
Those Lanes with walls of stone,
Did you run or wander and roam.
Could you see the smoke from the railway,
Rise over the Kingdom of Fife,
Have you stood on Ladybank station,
Was it happy your childhood life.
The Lomond Hills stand high,
As high as the Scottish sky.
Is that where you wanted to be,

Did you want to climb them to see,
North to the Firth of Tay,
The church of Collessie or Cupar,
And out to St. Andrews bay.
Did you ever ride out to the ocean,
Watch the fishing boats mooring at Crail,
Was the sea your only tomorrow,
How soon were you likely to sail.
Your bloodline runs on now in England,
Bennet Kennedy roots lie in Fife,
We honour the land we are living,
But The Kingdoms a part of our life.

It's not only a feeling in England but also when in Scotland; a calling, inside of me to be in Fife. Driving over the border near Gretna is a fantastic feeling for me. For the next hour and a half I see the road signs to Glasgow and Edinburgh and the towns before there. The Forth is on my mind and a strong desire to cross over, or to be by it at South Queensferry, from there Fife is in view.

As of yet the new crossing is not complete but becoming near. What will that feeling be for me? The welcome sign that's visible at the end of the older bridge lifts the heart, the new one will no doubt do so too.

Questions are being asked; take the coast road and park up by the Forth and admire the view? No! Come to Kirkcaldy as soon as you can Robbie, you've good reason to? Whichever way we decide it's just a magnificent ancestral feeling to be back in Fife.

So I get accustomed to the week or so that we are up there and have a couple of drives out of the kingdom. Once again road signs make their presence known. I immediately know when I am crossing the boundary. Fife is like a concerned parent watching over the bairn allowed to go somewhere without them for the first time. It's like a partner in a marriage and one is going to a place without the other. Trusting, hoping that they stay faithful. Then comes the moment on our return drive that I see the welcome sign; most often I read it out in a Scottish accent; if not, I think it.

I'll never know the answer, but not long before dad died, he went back. I had been contacted to say that he was in Dunfermline. In those days I didn't even know where in Scotland that was, did he have th' callin' o' Fife?

'a feeling, there in the heart,
deep in the mind
an underestimation of strength
of th' Callin' o' Fife'

So to draw in on this latest literary composition of poetic fact and fiction; I need to think hard if it's worth it; such as the early starts and five hour drive. Surely it would easier to drive west to Wales or south to Devon and Cornwall which has picturesque views and coastline. Travel east to Norfolk where we had memorable childhood holidays. The downside in my mind is because my roots are not there which must be important to me.

This 'Staffordshire Poet' writes these words in the conservatory of his Codsall home. He hadn't noticed until he placed his cup down; his drink was in a Fife cup on a Dundee place mat. I thought back to that first trip to Fife in 2002 and questioned myself once more as to why I didn't go earlier in life?

Fifteen years later being in Kirkcaldy to commemorate the 100 years of the death of Private Alexander Kennedy. It was in Kirkcaldy that this man arrived at the Cherrydene Guest House on the Bennochy Road in 2002 to have his first sleep in Fife.

The same month of April 2017 brings another 100 years when my Wolverhampton grandfather Benjamin James Owen, Isaiah's son, was injured in France. He became a member of the Territorial Army reserve in 1915 and was mobilised in the 4th Battalion of the Lincolnshire Regiment on 12 April 1916.

We have information that he was wounded on 25 April 1917, after being captured and trying to escape. This was witnessed by a neighbour who apparently was also in the same regiment. He crawled about the battlefield for four days, drinking water from the bottles of the dead. He was spotted by French Officers and was picked-up. His injuries were to his shoulder and his one lung. He was treated in Northumberland War Hospital, Bosworth, in Newcastle-on-Tyne, being admitted on 19 May 1917 and discharged on 11 February 1918.

Benjamin James Owen returned to Sarah Ann and their son Benjamin Joseph Owen. They were to go on to have another 5 children, the last being my mother in 1929.
Unfortunately Sarah Ann was to die of pneumonia a few weeks after she was born. This resulted in my mother being adopted by her newly-wed Aunt and Uncle. Benjamin James Owen re-married and lived on until 1935 when he also died of pneumonia.

So the memories fade of imagining William Wallace on that road through Fife to Perth and then Mary Queen of Scots escaping at Loch Leven and again as she walks out of that door near the ruins of St Andrews.

Now Lady Wulfruna opens her arms and welcomes me back home to Wolverhampton.

A day later a two year old great grandson of a Fifer couldn't get his Scotland rugby shirt on quick enough; it was bought for him in his ancestral Dundee. He then kicks a Scotland football that's a present of his 6 month old cousin; a picture that would be at home in 'Studio Bennetto.'

'lang may yer lum reek'

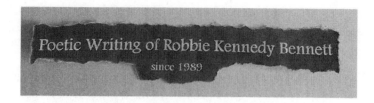

More Books by the Author

Awa' th' Rough Hills an' Awa';

I consider my poetic writing to be short story odes amongst a bigger picture of life. It is not chapter to chapter writing but story and reason to the rhyme.

Childhood memories of the area that had an input into my growing-up years leading into youthful days, courtship, married life and parenthood.

This book will take the reader on a poetic journey to the days when the fields near to the Monkey House and Rough Hills Tavern had youngsters playing and the pubs were a hub of activity.

All in the life of boy to man, who was raised on the Rough Hills Estate of Wolverhampton. In recent years my writing has reached my ancestral Scotland with becoming a featured poet.

Wulfrunian Footprints in Fife;

My poetic ancestral journey from my Wulfrunian upbringing to The Kingdom of Fife in Scotland.

Inspired by the land of my late dad, a Fifer who met my mother in Aldershot Military Hospital in the late1940's, married and settled in Wolverhampton. Fife was to become part of my life, walking the Fife Coastal Path and climbing the Lomond Hills, whilst searching my Scottish family roots.

From the inland villages of Collesie and Ladybank, to coastal towns of Kirkcaldy and St Andrews then over the Tay to Dundee, another ancestral home. Being where my dad and his forefathers may have worked and lived gave a great inspiration to the writing of this book. All this and more in picture, story and ode by this man of thought and sometimes thoughtless Wulfrunian.

'Ode' Gold Wolves;

An illustrated collection of my poems related to Wolverhampton Wanderers Football Club, well known as Wolves. Having been born in Wolverhampton of English and Scottish parentage, I grew up to have Wolves at heart.

Within a week of my arrival on this earth in 1954, Wolves were crowned First Division Champions. I was raised on the Rough Hills Estate area of Wolverhampton and could hear the roar of the Molineux crowd whenever a goal was scored. It never ceases to amaze me as to where next I shall find a supporter of Wolves.

Kicking around Codsall;

My descriptive poetic writing from our time as a family living in Codsall, Staffordshire, north west of Wolverhampton since 1986. There has been endless dog walks and training runs for me over the fields and down lanes that surround what we call the village. I soon felt part of the community of Codsall due to actively taking part in the games of football on the village hall playing field. Having being a writer of poems and odes for over a quarter of a century, it was time to see if I had enough work to produce a book with a Codsall theme. People, places, sunrises and life events are a few reasons as to why my verses are created.

Jock I've Been to Hampden;

I can still recall the overwhelming feeling when first experiencing the atmosphere of a crowded Hampden Park and the ancestral pride in being there. Scotland and football has always been of interest because of my parentage. The first time at Hampden I recall looking at the Scottish flags flying over the opposite stand and at the rooftops of the buildings of Glasgow. I was there for Bennet's of Fife and Dundee, Traill of St Andrews and Kennedy of Kirkcaldy and more.

Odes related to Scottish football, professional, grass roots or whatever. All because I have an ancestral interest. To experience Scottish Cup Finals and Internationals and wishing that I had played in Scotland myself when a young man. From day one Scottish footballers have always been of interest to me. It must be in the blood.

On a Wolverhampton Journey;

Memories in description, picture and ode of growing up and living in Wolverhampton. Many of the roads I have run in my days of training for the marathon and travelled on to my places of employment. My growing up and then youthful courting years to marriage, parenthood and home loving life. An active sporting man who turned out to be a very thoughtful person by writing many story poems which the Black Country Bugle were first to print. On a Wolverhampton Journey is a local poetic insight into my travel through the stages of my life to the present day.

The decision to go ahead with this book was because of Aw' th' Rough Hills an' Away. This being my first book appears to be of local interest. From there my Wulfrunian Footprints in Fife was featured in a Scottish newspaper. 'Ode' Gold Wolves, our local football club where former times and players are remembered. Kicking around Codsall was my contribution to the village where I now live.

I have often said that I was not a great scholar in the classroom, therefore to get close to having work published in my name was a fantastic feeling. I have always had an imaginative mind and can easily drift away into thought.

People, places and memories inspired this wanderer to write more work to publish this book of Wolverhampton, my hometown.

Back an' Forth;

My second book about my poetic ancestral journey from my Wulfrunian upbringing to the Kingdom of Fife in Scotland.

Drawn down the path of my dad and our bloodline to villages such as Collessie and Ladybank and to the coastal towns of Kirkcaldy and St Andrews. This is a continuous story that developed after the passing of my late dad. Delving into my roots brought a fascination of life and events in their time that I creatively write about. 'Wulfrunian Footprints in Fife' set the ball rolling and continues with this book 'Back an' Forth tae Fife.'

In 2014 came 25 years of writing in which over a decade of that had included a Scottish theme. This being as I was influenced greatly by this historic county of Scotland. The characteristic of the coast and landscape brought inspiration to many of the writings. As I have grown older my appreciation of Fife is a proud ancestral inheritance.

The odes within are heartfelt and warming that will take you back to a past that included my Fife ancestors. My imaginative mind created poems of the time of my forefathers in the land of theirs that they lived. New generations have now made this journey back to their roots ensuring that our Fife connection will continue in mind and spirit.

Poetic Writing of

Robbie Kennedy Bennett

Amazon have an Author page that you may wish to visit
or my website of the above name.

18856704R10172

Printed in Poland
by Amazon Fulfillment
Poland Sp. z o.o., Wrocław